A BRIEF GUIDE TO

MARITIME
STRATEGY

A BRIEF GUIDE TO

MARITIME STRATEGY

JAMES R. HOLMES

Naval Institute Press
Annapolis, Maryland

Naval Institute Press
291 Wood Road
Annapolis, MD 21402

Library of Congress Cataloging-in-Publication Data

Names: Holmes, James Ronald, 1965– author.
Title: A brief guide to maritime strategy / James R. Holmes.
Description: Annapolis : Naval Institute Press, 2019. | Includes
    bibliographical references and index.
Identifiers: LCCN 2019029384 (print) | LCCN 2019029385 (ebook) |
    ISBN 9781682473818 (paperback) | ISBN 9781682473825 (pdf) |
    ISBN 9781682473825 (epub)
Subjects: LCSH: Naval strategy.
Classification: LCC V163 .H65 2019 (print) | LCC V163 (ebook) |
    DDC 359/.03—dc23
LC record available at https://lccn.loc.gov/2019029384
LC ebook record available at https://lccn.loc.gov/2019029385

♾ Print editions meet the requirements of ANSI/NISO z39.48-1992
(Permanence of Paper).

Printed in the United States of America.

27 26 25 24 23 22 21 20 19   9 8 7 6 5 4 3 2 1
First printing

Contents

Foreword

The "end state" in "A Design for Maintaining Maritime Superiority," version 2.0, is to create "a dominant naval force that produces outstanding leaders and teams, armed with the best equipment, that learn and adapt faster than our rivals." To achieve this end state in a contest with great powers, the U.S. Navy, Marine Corps, and Coast Guard must compete and win against "near peer" armed forces—forces comparable to our own in technology, skill, and numbers—and do so far forward, often in our rivals' home waters. But there's so much to achieving this end state!

We need to reach this goal not in general terms but in very specific terms. We must produce *actual* leaders and teams—recruit, educate, train, and retain them. As well, we must arm them with *actual* equipment—innovate, research, experiment, produce, and distribute. And perhaps most important, we must apply these against *specific* rivals—capabilities, politics, techniques, and geography. While some things will apply in general to all cases, one size definitely does not fit all. Each rival requires a tailored plan of ideas and capabilities to connect our naval forces to our political aims. This is strategy.

Today the need for clear strategic thinking is acute. In order to make progress, the naval officer corps needs a common baseline—perspective and vocabulary—to identify and debate courses of action meant to help achieve strategic advantage. That means *all* officers, from newly commissioned ensigns and second lieutenants to senior admirals and generals, need to be familiar with the strategic canon. Professor Holmes has done a great service to help us achieve this fluency.

By introducing the central ideas from the masters of maritime strategy—Mahan, Corbett, and their kindred theorists—and by doing so in an accessible way, I believe this book will help officers, especially junior officers, attain a working knowledge in larger strategic things while still having the time to attend to their demanding duties becoming tactical experts. Combining the dynamism and energy of youth with a knowledge of maritime strategy will better equip the Navy, Marine Corps, and Coast Guard to prevail over our rivals and secure the open, accessible, rules-based world order on which our influence and prosperity depend.

ADMIRAL JOHN M. RICHARDSON
U.S. Navy (retired)

Preface
A Lifelong Enterprise

This book is a tutorial for my younger self. In 1987, fresh out of Naval ROTC at Vanderbilt, I was a novice in the profession of arms. That did not last. Newly commissioned naval officers are reared on tactical and technical matters. Yet one thing was missing from all that schooling— namely, acquaintanceship with the purposes that steaming around the seven seas, firing weapons, or hobnobbing with folk in foreign lands were meant to serve. Naval training was silent on topics that fell beyond the daily grind of administration, equipment maintenance, and watchstanding. Nor did assignment to the fleet correct that deficit. Just the opposite. Sea duty left even less time for extracurricular reading—let alone a self-education in larger things.

This is no indictment. Nor is this educational deficit peculiar to the U.S. Navy. It is common to all modern navies. Prime Minister and two-time First Lord of the Admiralty Winston Churchill bewailed the state of strategic knowledge and insight in Great Britain's Royal Navy during the age of steam: "The seafaring and scientific technique of the naval profession makes such severe demands upon the training of naval men, that they have very rarely the time or opportunity to study military history and the art of war in general."[1] Now as then, naval warfare is an intensely technical affair. Then, mariners sought to master steam engineering plants, gunnery, and fire control. Today their successors must master all of that plus missile and aviation technology, advanced sensors and computers, and, increasingly, such esoteric fields as cyberwarfare and artificial intelligence. Time remains the stern tyrant that it was in Churchill's day.

This book represents an effort to help newcomers to the sea services cope with the tyranny of time. It is a primer on maritime strategy, and like all primers it is short. Humorist Mark Twain once wisecracked that he had written a long speech because he had no time to write a short one. Twain meant it is possible to concentrate the essence of a topic into a few words rather than ramble on at length. (He also meant it takes extra effort to prune away the excess.) This book constitutes my effort to condense the rudiments of maritime strategy—those larger purposes propelling endeavors on the high seas—into something a junior officer, congressional staffer, or newly minted graduate student in international security might find a few scarce hours to read. It will enrich their perspective on operational assignments while preparing them for more intensive study of the subject at midcareer, when officers matriculate at professional military education institutes or civilian universities.

So much for what this book is. What is it *not*? First, it is not all-encompassing. Maritime strategy is a genre of "grand" strategy. It helps the topmost leadership of an outward-facing, trade-oriented country such as the United States fashion national goals, accumulate the wherewithal to attain those goals, and put diplomatic, economic, and military resources to work attaining them. At the same time maritime strategy is subsidiary to a much broader field of strategy. Readers will look in vain for much mention of ground combat, air power, cyberwarfare, or other disciplines not intimately related to seagoing trade, commerce, and military endeavors. These things are important, often critically so. But keeping this book short and digestible demanded hard decisions about what to include and what to exclude.

That being the case, much of the strategic canon is absent. Prussian soldier Carl von Clausewitz and Chinese master Sun Tzu, generally acclaimed within the U.S. professional military education establishment as history's foremost strategic thinkers, put in only cursory appearances here. They have little if anything to say exclusively about the sea. Non-Western scribes such as Kautilya, ancient India's predominant theorist of statecraft, or Mao Zedong, whose strategy of "active defense" remains the core of Communist Chinese military strategy, likewise ended up on the cutting-room floor. This book is far from the last word on strategy. I hope it constitutes a good first word about maritime strategy and a platform for future study and meditation.

Second, tactics are altogether absent from this volume. Crudely speaking, I conceive of the book as a companion to Capt. Wayne Hughes' *Fleet Tactics*, a work first published when I was a midshipman.[2] This book provides an inkling of why merchantmen and warships venture out across the main; Captain Hughes explains how tacticians should conduct themselves in times of crisis or war. There is no substitute for knowing strategy *and* tactics. After all, strategists and policymakers untutored in tactics have a fateful habit of writing checks that tacticians cannot cash. Tacticians unfamiliar with strategy have only a foggy sense of what top leadership expects them to accomplish. They are apt to underperform without an understanding of larger purposes. In short, there is much ruin in the disjuncture between the strategic and tactical levels. Closing it is a focal point of military education.

Third, this is not some dispassionate survey of the subject. Still less is it a digest of everything the greats—the Alfred Thayer Mahans and Julian Corbetts—had to say about transacting business in great waters. A bibliography of Mahan's writings is itself a book.[3] Corbett compiled a body of work that is somewhat less formidable in girth yet arguably exceeds it in insight. Instead these are my views about maritime strategy after a quarter-century of studying it. I take a plug-and-play approach to maritime strategy: I believe it possible to look to Mahan's teachings for insight into political and strategic purpose yet look to other writers for guidance on how to use sea power to fulfill Mahanian purposes. Not everyone agrees with this way of looking at things.

Readers must immerse themselves in the classics over the course of a career and make up their own minds about such matters. They may disagree, and there is nothing wrong with that. In fact, creative discord does martial institutions good. It reveals the full range of courses of action for a given set of circumstances while exposing strengths, weaknesses, and fallacies underlying the arguments for any particular course of action. It helps commanders or their political superiors make decisions with the fullest possible information and insight. It keeps an institution fresh and nimble in the midst of galloping change.

A note on how to use this volume: consult the endnotes. I went heavy on them not just because of the usual scholarly hygiene but to provide supplemental reading recommendations. They are designed to help newcomers to maritime strategy start branching out into what interests them and might prove useful in their careers. Look up a reference, read the text to either side of the passage quoted, and see where it takes you.

Since Clausewitz is a bit player in ensuing chapters, it is fitting for him to have the last word here. Strategy is not about compiling manuals, algorithms, or checklists that guarantee victory. That is a sterile if all too common way of looking at the profession of arms and a sure way to court defeat at the hands of more dynamic foes. Rather, he proclaims, strategic theory "exists so that one need not start afresh each time sorting out the material and plowing through it."[4] Theory provides a frame of reference. Knowing it spares officers and officials from having to start from scratch thinking through problems that great minds such as Clausewitz, or Mahan, or Corbett have already thought through.

Reading about strategy and military history, declares Clausewitz, "is meant to educate the mind of the future commander, or, more accurately, *to guide him in his self-education* . . . just as a wise teacher guides and stimulates a young man's intellectual development, but is careful not to lead him by the hand for the rest of his life" (my emphasis).[5] Clausewitz sounds marvelously modern here. Nowadays academicians tout the wonders of "lifelong learning," whereby graduates take ownership of their own reading and learning after they depart the schoolhouse. Self-education never ends.

Posterity has nothing on the long-dead Prussian, who grasped the virtue of lifelong learning many decades before the slogan was invented. This book will be worthwhile if it helps junior folk commence educating themselves sooner than I did—and furthers the lifelong project of which Clausewitz wrote so eloquently. The views voiced in this book are mine alone.

Chapter 1 | How to Generate
Sea Power

Maritime strategy is the art and science of using power to fulfill purposes relating to the sea. Sea power is a means to the strategic ends set by political leaders in concert with domestic constituents. Alfred Thayer Mahan will help guide this survey of maritime strategy, joined from time to time by other greats in the field. Mahan was a fin de siècle American sea captain and arguably history's most influential historian and theorist of nautical affairs. He was the first strategy professor at the Naval War College in Newport, Rhode Island, not to mention the college's second president.[1] His words carry weight.

But first a caveat is in order. Nowadays Mahan is remembered as an "evangelist" of titanic sea fights and the big-gun battleships used to wage them.[2] In this telling the oceans and seas are simply a battleground where fleets pummel one another in their quest to rule the waves. Mahan is best known for defining "command of the sea" as "overbearing power on the sea which drives the enemy's flag from it, or allows it to appear only as a fugitive."[3] *Overbearing* power—that sounds definitive. Maritime strategy, it seems, is entirely a martial thing. It's all about ships blasting away at one another on the wine-dark sea.

Such renderings do Mahan a disservice. True, he recounts sea fights from the age of sail in exacting if not wearisome detail. The military factor features prominently in his writings. Yet he does not depict fighting as an end in itself. It is a means for national self-preservation. Self-preservation constitutes the "first law of states," he writes, while national growth is "a property of healthful life." The natural right to growth bestows a right to protect progress by force of arms, deploying military or naval power should some rival "overpass its own lawful sphere." Seagoing societies must arm for self-defense lest a foe inject the "alien element" of armed force into peaceful seaborne commerce from which they prosper.[4]

So it turns out that maritime strategy is not about battle for its own sake after all. For Mahan a navy is simply a backstop for diplomatic efforts to open, nourish, and safeguard commercial access to important trading theaters such as East Asia and Western Europe. War is not his means of choice. In fact, he avers, it "has ceased to be the natural, or even normal, condition of nations."[5] Military might is "simply accessory and subordinate to the other greater interests, economical and commercial."[6]

The goal of a Mahanian maritime strategy, then, is "to secure commerce, by political measures conducive to military, or naval, strength. This order is that of *actual relative importance* to the nation of the three elements—*commercial, political, military*" (my emphasis).[7] Maritime strategy is about access. Its paramount goal is commercial access. Governments seek diplomatic access to promote commercial access. And military access supports diplomacy by force of arms, should commercial access come under duress from foreign competitors.

Thus, commerce is king in the Mahanian order of things. Maritime strategy means harnessing sea power to support diplomacy—and thence commercial access and the economic prosperity it brings. In turn the navy is a beneficiary of prosperity since economic vitality generates the revenue the government needs to fund a navy. Setting in motion and sustaining this virtuous cycle among economics, diplomacy, and naval might is what maritime strategy is all about. Girding for battle is a subsidiary though inescapable function.

The ancients would agree. In his classic *History of the Peloponnesian War*, the chronicler Thucydides reports that both Athenian and Spartan leaders agreed on the transcendent importance of economics and finance. The Spartan king Archidamus maintained that "war is a matter not so much of arms as of money, which makes arms of use." In other words, an armed host can possess an imposing panoply of weaponry yet accomplish little on the battlefield. It demands regular resupply of food and war-making matériel of all kinds to sustain operations in the field. Without logistical support—and without the money to procure it in bulk—the military machine sputters and eventually comes to a halt.

Economics, added Archidamus, was doubly crucial "in a struggle between a continental and a maritime power."[8] Maritime states are trading states. Their governments levy taxes to reap the bounty of international commerce. Seagoing Athens thus commanded a key advantage in the coming war against continental Sparta: it could fund a dominant fleet and keep it at sea for long stretches of time. Athenian "first citizen" Pericles concurred with his foe. "Capital," he proclaimed, "maintains a war," and thus the principal "hindrance" bedeviling Spartans was their "want of money."[9]

Mahan could scarcely agree more. Economic and financial vibrancy constitutes both the goal and the chief enabler of sea power. This is doubly true in times of protracted strategic competition or war. Statesmen and naval officialdom neglect the economic sinews of maritime strategy and operations at their peril.

What Is the Sea?

Before delving more deeply into the nature and uses of sea power, it is important to consider what the sea *is* as a strategic entity. This is part of knowing the surroundings. Let's classify the sea as a maritime "common"; a medium for human interaction, both competitive and cooperative; a unified whole in time and space; a featureless plain on the open ocean; a borderland broken by terrain once ships approach the coast; a three-dimensional domain where submarines and aircraft can roam; and an environment that molds how seafarers and aviators think about their professions. It is far from a simple two-dimensional plane across which ships travel from point A to point B.

The Sea as a Maritime Common

In part the oceans are what human beings define them to be. Mahan was first to label the sea a "wide common" or "great common." He portrayed it as "a great highway," or better, "a wide common, over which men may pass in all directions, but on which some well-worn paths show that controlling reasons have led them to choose certain lines of travel rather than others. These lines of travel are called trade routes."[10] But while Mahan formulated the metaphor, the idea of a nautical common dates from long before his lifetime. In fact, it originated as an international legal concept. Designating some physical space as a common denotes that it belongs to everyone and to no one. It is an ungoverned or lightly governed space open to free use by all. Nearly untrammeled freedom prevails.

Think about the New England town common. In Revolutionary times the common was a green space where cattle or sheep could graze, sporting events could be held, or cemeteries or parks could be built.[11] Town leaders could set aside a common without controversy because the town exercised "sovereignty" over that parcel of land. No one could gainsay its authority to allocate territory how it saw fit. German sociologist Max Weber, who appears from time to time in this volume, furnishes the classic definition of sovereignty. Weber describes a sovereign as "a human community that (successfully) claims the *monopoly of the legitimate use of physical force* within a given territory" (emphasis in original).[12] The sovereign makes rules and laws within its borders and backs them with physical force in the form of police and armed services, and citizens obey the rules and laws or face legal repercussions.

The marine common is a more complex entity than the New England town common of yore. For one thing, there is no sovereign of the seas. Oceans do not lie within the unambiguous jurisdiction of any coastal state. They adjoin jurisdictions ruled by sovereigns. Governments see different interests at stake in the saltwater domain and may enact policies and laws that conflict with those instituted by their neighbors. For another, there are physical limits to any navy's capacity to enforce a genuine monopoly on the use of force throughout the empty vastness of the world's oceans and seas. Unlike a municipal police force that can enforce dominion within compact city limits, the biggest navy is tiny by comparison with the territory it must oversee. Physical space dilutes its strength.

Accordingly, seagoing states long bickered over the extent to which any individual state can make itself sovereign over the oceans. Seventeenth-century jurists Hugo Grotius and John Selden are the two faces of this debate. Grotius, a Dutchman, penned an anonymous tract in 1608 contending that no state may claim dominion over the maritime common.[13] Grotius was defending Dutch merchants' right to trade in the Indian Ocean. The Portuguese Empire sought to bar access to that expanse to uphold its monopoly on trade. Selden, an Englishman, countered both that coastal sovereigns *could* own the sea—sovereignty being the counterpart to public or private ownership in the domestic sphere—and that England held rightful title to "the British Sea, or that which encompasses the life of Great Britain."[14] Published in 1652, Selden's treatise constituted his belated reply to Grotius. Selden countered for fear that the doctrine of freedom of the sea would set at naught the English Crown's prerogatives in the North Atlantic.

Who won the argument between proponents of free and closed seas? Until recent years it appeared Grotius had come out on top by acclamation. The second of President Woodrow Wilson's "Fourteen Points," which set forth principles for the peace settlement ending World War I, commits adherents to "absolute freedom of navigation upon the seas, outside territorial waters, alike in peace and in war."[15] Today the UN Convention on the Law of the Sea (UNCLOS), the closest thing the seafaring world has to a "constitution of the oceans," strives to reconcile Selden's doctrine of the closed sea with Grotius' vision of the free sea. Nevertheless, the balance its framers struck overwhelmingly favors the idea that the sea is a common. The convention apportions a narrow belt of water just off a coastal state's shores to that state as its "territorial sea." The coastal state exercises full sovereignty there, making laws and regulations governing what ships and planes may do. Under the doctrine of "innocent passage," foreign ships may skirt through the territorial sea provided they forgo all military activities.[16]

Selden's vision reigns in that strip of water but nowhere else. The territorial sea extends 12 nautical miles offshore. Beyond territorial waters lies another 12-mile belt, the "contiguous zone," where coastal states may enforce customs, fiscal, immigration, and sanitary laws and regulations. And beyond that lies the exclusive economic zone (EEZ), which extends 200 nautical miles offshore, or sometimes up to 350 nautical miles where the continental shelf juts out that far. As the term implies, UNCLOS entitles coastal states to absolute rights to harvest natural resources from the seabed or the water within the EEZ.[17] They enjoy no other special rights there.

Beyond the EEZ lie the high seas, an ungoverned space with a few exceptions codified by treaty. The Convention for the Suppression of Unlawful Acts Against the Safety of Maritime Navigation, to name one such accord, sets forth some of the exceptions—notably, procedures for apprehending, trying, and punishing pirates.[18] Vessels may travel hither and yon across the high seas, conducting such military, commercial, and scientific activities as they please. In other words, freedom of the sea—Grotius' paradigm—prevails beyond twelve nautical miles from land, with severely limited exceptions in the contiguous zone and EEZ. The oceans remain a marine common. Seafaring states reaffirmed it by enacting UNCLOS.

And while the U.S. Senate has declined to consent to the convention, presidential administrations from both parties have accepted it as "customary" international law, a type of unwritten law grounded in the "practice of states." Customary international law exists alongside treaty law, much as common law coexists with written laws in many domestic legal systems. In other words, what states do—their observable behavior—indicates what they believe international law and norms to be.

The near-universal membership of UNCLOS carries weight. It supplies compelling evidence of how signatories view the law of the sea. In short, America has an awkward relationship with the law of the sea: it stands outside the written constitution of the oceans yet also happens to be its chief enforcer. The U.S. Navy routinely challenges extralegal maritime claims under the U.S. State Department's Freedom of Navigation program.[19] U.S. mariners and their political masters must manage this awkwardness on a daily basis.

The law of the sea seemed to have become settled international law until 2009, when China proclaimed "indisputable sovereignty" within a "nine-dashed line," or sometimes "ten-dashed line," on the map of the South China Sea. The nine-dashed line encloses an estimated 80–90 percent of this vital waterway. Beijing commenced demanding that ships transiting the region abide by the rules of innocent passage, and it constructed artificial island fortresses to back its demands with firepower.[20] In effect, it started treating the Southeast Asian common as its territorial sea.

Selden has returned from his intellectual exile with a vengeance and taken up residence in Beijing. The international consensus favoring maritime liberty could prove perishable after all if influential coastal states apply diplomatic and military power to oppose it and no one pushes back often or effectively enough. It is worth noting that international law can evolve. If a coastal state makes an extraordinary claim and fellow seafaring states comply with it over time, it could come to qualify as an international custom and, ultimately, as customary law.

Sometimes states do acquiesce in extralegal claims. In 1823 the United States proclaimed the Monroe Doctrine, a unilateral policy statement whereby Washington purported to regulate what European empires could and could not do in the Western Hemisphere. To oversimplify, it forbade Europeans to reconquer American states that had won their independence.[21] But although the Monroe Doctrine was never international law, few Europeans saw much interest in expending serious diplomatic and naval resources to challenge it. As a result the doctrine came to qualify as an international custom. America made a unilateral statement and others conformed to it for decades. The Versailles Treaty terminating World War I stops short of affirming that the Monroe Doctrine is international law, but it explicitly affirms the doctrine's standing as a "regional [understanding] . . . for securing the maintenance of peace."[22]

A kind of quasi-legal status came to imbue this axiom of U.S. foreign policy. A similar process could grant China's nine-dashed line de facto legal standing should the seafaring world fail to challenge it. English common law guarantees citizens the "right-of-way," meaning the right to use certain pathways across private property so long as people actually avail themselves of that right. The right-of-way loses force if no one uses it over time. Freedom of the sea could likewise cease to exist in part or in whole if no one exercises it regularly. Laws affirming access to physical space can die through neglect.

Nor are the ramifications of this quarrel confined to a single body of water, troublesome though it would be to see the South China Sea closed. If Beijing successfully upholds the nine-dashed line, establishing the principle that the Chinese Communist Party makes the rules governing maritime movement and others must comply, Beijing will have chipped away at freedom of the sea not just in Southeast Asia but in other peripheral bodies of water across the globe. It will have set a dangerous precedent. Freedom of the sea is indivisible. Its principles apply in full, everywhere, or they are at risk everywhere. If China annuls the law of the sea in Southeast Asia, other coastal states could act on that precedent, asserting dominion over seaways such as the Black Sea, Sea of Azov, or Baltic Sea.

The twenty-first century is witnessing the ghosts of Selden and Grotius square off anew. The maritime common could contract if proponents of closed seas—latter-day acolytes of Selden—back their claims with hardheaded diplomacy and superior firepower. It behooves friends of nautical freedom to take league with Grotius. They must press their case early and often for continuing to define the common *as* a common and must think ahead about how to use military might to renovate and sustain Grotius' vision.

The new, old debate about freedom of the sea may signify that debates over policy or law are not forever won or lost. If China believes it can impose a monopoly of force within a major artery like the South China Sea, then it may indeed harbor the conceit that it can make itself sovereign there.

Grudging acceptance of the new reality might follow as rival claimants realize they can do nothing about it. A modicum of legitimacy might come to surround China's claims over time—and Beijing would have approximated sovereignty by Max Weber's standard.

The Sea as a Medium for Human Interaction

Surveying the argument about open and closed seas reveals that the oceans are a medium for human interactions ranging from amicable cooperation to high-seas war. Emeritus King's College London professor Geoffrey Till explores the nature and uses of the sea, fashioning a simple yet powerful model of four "historic attributes of the sea"—resources, transportation, information, and dominion—that helps practitioners think through topics relating to maritime cooperation and conflict.[23]

Each of Till's attributes conveys a basic function of the sea. The sea and seabed constitute a reservoir of natural resources such as fish, oil and gas, and minerals. In the spirit of Grotius and Mahan, Till observes that the oceans comprise a common or a highway beyond any coastal state's legal jurisdiction. Seagoing nations can transport commercial goods and military forces along this oceanic thoroughfare to reach any other seaport across the globe. The sea offers a forum for cultural interchange. And it is an arena where sovereign states may struggle for control of important expanses or rimlands.[24]

Till postulates that each attribute of the sea is either wholly cooperative or competitive in character, or that some composite of cooperation and competition typifies it. Naval endeavors represent such a compound. Military competition raises the prospect that one contestant might try to get its way by force of arms. But at the same time the multifaceted nature of naval power complicates efforts to distinguish between competitive and collaborative missions. Tanks, fighter jets, and artillery pieces are warfighting implements. They do little else. Warships serve multiple purposes. A ship of war can render humanitarian or disaster assistance, apprehend gunrunners or human traffickers, promote goodwill in foreign seaports, or prosecute a myriad of other noncombat missions. Or, obviously, it can wage war.

Intent is what alters a warship's character. Orders received from senior commanders and their political masters determine whether the vessel discharges pacific or more warlike functions. Nor is there much way to predict the nature of its duties from moment to moment. Orders can change. A warship dispatched on an errand of mercy could revert to its combat function almost instantly if so directed. Conceivably, it could even turn its weapons on its partners from a minute ago.

In this vein strategist Edward Luttwak observes that a fleet's battle capability "can be activated at any time, while the formulation of the intent" to do so can be "both silent and immediate." Even "routine fleet movements which [are] not intended to pose a threat may be seen by others as threatening (since the threat is *latent* in the forces themselves)" (emphasis in original).[25] This is less true of lightly armed coast guards, while nonmilitary maritime agencies are even less menacing. The choice of instrument for a mission matters.

By definition, dominion is the most competitive among Till's four attributes. If one power or alliance commands vital expanses for its own parochial purposes, it could exclude others—restricting their ability to use the sea-lanes or exploit natural resources. Contests for dominion—or the fear of such contests—could act as a spoiler for more collaborative endeavors that bring seagoing states together. Chapter 3 says much more about dominion, the province of maritime military strategy, and about how to derive political value from fleet deployments.

Till's first attribute of the sea, resources, appears less competitive than dominion. As noted before, UNCLOS allocates an EEZ to each coastal state for its sole use.[26] UNCLOS also establishes a cooperative regime for jointly extracting resources from the seabed in international waters, should such efforts become profitable and technologically feasible.[27] Cooperation prevails so long as coastal states abide by the law of the sea.

But maritime territorial boundaries remain disputed in many waterways. Quarrels over natural resources in disputed zones commonly prove intractable. After all, national well-being suffers without access to offshore resources. This is the case in the South China Sea, where multiple claimants assert title to islands and the adjacent waters and China claims virtually the whole expanse.[28] Feuding over where to demarcate territorial seas, contiguous zones, and EEZs thus constitutes another potential spoiler for "good order at sea," Till's phrase for constabulary work meant to keep the sea safe for mercantile shipping.[29] It could even fuel struggles for dominion, setting strife in motion between coastal states intent on economic development.

Till's information function is elemental yet overlooked in maritime affairs. Seafaring is a medium for cultural interaction and exchanges of information. Such exchanges occur in the course of things. Sailors mingle with peoples they encounter while tarrying in foreign ports of call. Journalist Robert Kaplan goes so far as to suggest that such interchange modulates—and moderates—the cultures of coastal societies relative to their inland neighbors.[30]

But there is far more to the information function than incidental cultural exchange—a byproduct of mixing with coastal peoples. The information domain is also a medium where naval officialdom communicates messages that support foreign policy, displays impressive implements of sea power, and telegraphs resolve to cow opponents, hearten allies and friends, and recruit new partners for common undertakings. Mariners strive to use this medium to shape opinion in favor of national purposes. The coming chapters have much more to say about "naval diplomacy."

Cooperative endeavors, then, are often limited to Till's transportation function, both because it is the least contentious and because common interests there are most obvious and compelling. Few coastal states have a stake in interrupting the free movement of merchantmen between suppliers and customers. Commerce, after all, is king. Safeguarding transportation networks appears the most amenable to multinational action among the four attributes. At the same time, it behooves governments to remember that they cannot easily compartment their maritime activities, partitioning off competitive undertakings from friendly collaboration. Multifaceted problems lurk when seafaring states undertake competitive and cooperative missions in the same waters. One can intersect with, distort, or ruin another.

The Sea as a Unified Whole in Time and Space

The world's oceans and seas are a single, unified body of water. In geophysical terms, Mahan portrays them as an indivisible whole. He deprecates commonplace yet largely arbitrary distinctions between various bodies of water. In all likelihood, then, he would agree with scholars' and governments' habit of depicting the Pacific Ocean and Indian Ocean as a grand "Indo-Pacific" theater.[31] Not only are the oceans and seas interconnected—with such obvious exceptions as the land-locked Caspian Sea—but they reach into the interiors of continents.[32] Navigable rivers are freshwater tendrils that place producers and consumers deep within the heartland in touch with the high seas, and thence with foreign markets and suppliers. Waterways such as the Mississippi River or Yangtze River expedite commerce and slash transaction costs by reducing the need for overland transport.

On the other hand, inland waterways pose dangers if not robustly defended. Foreign gunboats plied the Yangtze well into the twentieth century, exerting maritime might in

China's hinterlands.[33] Or as Mahan, a Union Navy veteran of the Civil War, points out in the American context: "the streams that had carried the wealth and supported the trade of the [Confederate states] turned against them, and admitted their enemies to their hearts."[34] With only a feeble navy to protect its shores and inland waters, the Confederacy lost control of those waterways—and saw itself dismembered from within. "Never," concludes Mahan, "did sea power play a greater or a more decisive part" than in the American Civil War.[35] Leaving the gate unbarred was imprudent in the extreme. Sea power is not for the high seas alone.

Oceans and seas are unified in other ways as well. Adm. James Stavridis, a former NATO supreme commander, opens his book *Sea Power* with a Mahanian-sounding appraisal of the sea's physical characteristics. He maintains that "the sea is one" not just in geographic space but in time. The world ocean sprawls "horizontally" across the globe, to be sure, but it also undulates "vertically" back in time. In other words, seafarers join something larger and older when they go down to the sea in ships. A sailor who walks out on deck sees "the same view, the same endless ocean that Alexander the Great saw as he sailed the eastern Mediterranean . . . and that Halsey saw as he lashed his Fast Carrier Task Force into combat in the western Pacific."[36]

Having served in one of Adm. "Bull" Halsey's Third Fleet surface combatants that was resurrected in the 1980s, I second these mystic-sounding words.[37] There *is* a connection with bygone generations of seafarers—and that bond forms part of interactions among American and foreign sailors. A mariner, attests Stavridis, is "at once an ocean away from the world of the land, but also connected to a long, unbroken chain of men and women who have set their course for the open ocean."[38] Seafaring folk partake of an oceanic fellowship spanning centuries.

The Sea as a Featureless Plain

The open ocean resembles a featureless plain. Mahan takes issue with the commonplace metaphor "sea-lanes." No roadways crisscross the sea. This terrestrial metaphor applies inexactly at best to the saltwater domain, implying that ships, like landbound conveyances such as trucks or automobiles, must traffic along predictable routes to journey from one place to another. And it implies that ships can be located—and, in wartime, detected, tracked, targeted, and attacked—along these routes. There is predictability and rhythm to seafaring.

Not so—or at least not *necessarily* so. Sea-lanes exist in that convenient routes do lead from one harbor to another. Taking the shortest route saves time, fuel, money, and wear and tear on crews and equipment. But the sea imposes no physical barrier to prevent seafarers from detouring onto more roundabout routes to avoid, say, rough weather, embattled or pirate-infested waters, or land conflicts that could spill seaward. Mahan likens the open sea to a flat plain where vector mechanics, not fixed terrain such as mountains or canyons, governs the movement of shipping:

> The sea, until it approaches the land, realizes the ideal of a vast plain unbroken by obstacles. On the sea . . . there is no field of battle, meaning that there [are] none of the natural conditions which determine, and often fetter, the movements of the general. . . . While in itself the ocean opposes no obstacle to a vessel taking any one of the numerous routes that can be traced upon the surface of the globe between two points, conditions of distance or convenience, of traffic or of wind, do prescribe certain usual courses.[39]

Instead of maps and landmarks, mariners use nautical charts, maneuvering boards that employ polar coordinates, and instruments familiar from geometry—compasses, sextants, parallel rulers, and the like—to navigate across this trackless surface. Since no impediments channel or block open-ocean movement, infinitely many sea routes connect a point along some seacoast with another point along some other seacoast.

Calling sea routes *lanes* thus misleads, as Mahan contends. Roadways simplify the problem of finding travelers on land. A police officer or highwayman has a good idea where to intercept motorists along some road. By contrast, a ship, submarine, or aircraft operating at sea must scour mostly vacant geographic space to find its quarry. The sea is colossal in size and volume, the largest ship or fleet puny by comparison. Commanders must disperse assets to monitor large sea areas—and it can prove nettlesome to gather those assets for action, combining their strength should the situation warrant. Maritime geography thus tends to attenuate physical power—whether the power of a coast guard policing the sea for lawbreakers or of a navy trying to vanquish some foe.

Still, finding one's quarry is not impossible. As Mahan points out, again, there are direct routes from one point to another, and ships tend to follow them. Because of the globe's spherical geometry, plotting a "great-circle track" often indicates the most economical pathway from point A to point B.[40] The economics of seafaring thus lends a measure of predictability to ship movements while abetting reconnaissance efforts. Mahan's contemporary, the English naval historian and theorist Sir Julian Corbett, reviews the practical aspects of finding vessels on the empty plain. Corbett divides the sea into "fertile areas" and "infertile areas." Fertile sea areas, he says, are densely populated with merchantmen—and thus are logical places for navies vying to control the sea to loiter. Shipping converges and congregates there while infertile areas remain largely vacant.[41]

Corbett explains that finding a ship is straightforward at only three points in its voyage: at its point of origin, at its destination, or at "focal points" or "focal areas" that it must traverse along its way. (Mahan concurs, adding that the port of origin is "the point at which a great maritime expedition, whether purely military or otherwise, can usually be most effectually watched."[42]) Focal areas are fertile areas. Sea routes come together at focal points where vessels pass through a strait or other narrow sea from one body of water into another.[43] Such entryways are saltwater counterparts to intersections on city streets. Vehicles approach an intersection from multiple directions and at multiple speeds. Traffic clusters there while passing through.

Both traffic intersections and maritime focal points help watchful police or military forces locate vehicles they wish to monitor or apprehend. The approaches to the Strait of Gibraltar, Strait of Hormuz, or Malacca Strait are just three of many focal areas scattered about the globe. For example, close to one hundred thousand vessels transit through Malacca every year, bearing some one-quarter of the world's trade goods.[44] Its approaches represent a quintessential fertile area in Corbett's parlance. And as China, India, the United States, and local powers jostle for power and influence in South and Southeast Asia, this focal point takes on geopolitical import as well.

The Sea as a Borderland Broken by Terrain Once Ships Approach the Coast

Corbett's logic of focal areas reveals that the sea comes to resemble a broken plain as a vessel closes in on shore. Terrain asserts itself there, just as the Rocky Mountains assert themselves along the western reaches of the Great Plains. It must be obeyed. Ships must yield to terrain where sea meets land or come to grief. Accordingly, it is a fallacy to make too much of the geometric nature of sea power. As noted before, Mahan rightly observes that the logic of the barren plain ruled by vector mechanics holds only until the sea "approaches the land."[45] Indeed, all three of Corbett's junctions for finding a ship—its origin, destination, and focal points—are found in places along the journey where open-ocean navigation must give way to immutable land features or meet an ill fate.

There *is* terrain at sea—chiefly at its landward edges. This is why ships "navigate" out on the open sea, using instruments and mathematical formulas to plot their positions and determine the proper courses and speeds, but "pilot" their way along the coasts. When piloting, their crews take visual sightings of shore features and navigational aids to fix their positions on the chart and steer clear of harm's way. Piloting resembles orienteering in important respects.

An old navy jest conveys this truism. An aircraft-carrier bridge watch team—or, according to some variants of the joke, the bridge team of a battleship—raises a contact on Channel 16, the VHF frequency designated for exchanging safety-related information at sea. The carrier skipper, presumably a senior sea dog mindful of the privileges of rank, demands that the other ship change course to avoid collision. Its master refuses to give way. Tempers flare. Eventually, after more parlaying, the unknown ship reveals itself to be . . . a lighthouse! "Your call," replies the lighthouse keeper when the flattop refuses to maneuver.[46] Land trumps sea where the twain meet. Sage maritime strategists, consequently, pay heed to geographic positions, critical bodies of water, and subsurface terrain.

The Sea as a Three-Dimensional Domain
Where Submarines and Aircraft Can Roam

The nautical common is a three-dimensional operating medium for specialized craft such as airplanes and submarines. Aircraft can maneuver for tactical advantage at various altitudes, while subs excel at hiding beneath oceanic layers and otherwise exploiting differentials in temperature, pressure, and salinity to confound enemy sensors and thus elude detection. They operate in volume rather than on a flat plain. There are limits even to this freedom, however. If the sea ceases to be a plain for surface craft close to shore, shallow water and narrow waterways channel and cramp submarines' freedom to maneuver. Aircraft likewise must obey immovable geographic features when taking off, landing, flying at low altitude over land, or cruising along the coast.

To advise seafarers, Mahan assembles a framework for assessing the strategic value and hazards of confined waterways such as straits. The approach is much like his formula for appraising sites for potential naval stations (covered in chapter 2). "The military importance of such passages or defiles," he says, "depends not only upon the geographical position but also upon their width, length, and difficulty." More specifically, a strait represents a "strategic point" whose value depends on its "situation," meaning its location on the nautical chart. Its value also turns on its "strength," meaning "the obstacles it puts in the way of an assailant and the consequent advantages to the holder."[47] To augment a strait's strength its occupant could strew obstacles such as sea mines in an enemy's path.

A narrow sea's value, furthermore, derives from "resources or advantages, such as the facility it gives the possessor for reaching a certain point."[48] Some passages are more important than others because of where they lie on the nautical chart. Mahan thus cautions against drawing conclusions about narrow seas without evaluating their larger geographic context. When "fixing the value of any passage," it is crucial to calculate the number and availability of nearby alternatives. "If so situated that a long circuit is imposed upon the belligerent who is deprived of its use, its value is enhanced." Scarcity magnifies a waterway's importance. Its value escalates if it constitutes "the only close link between two bodies of water, or two naval stations."[49]

A well-placed gateway shortens the distance from place to place for the contestant that holds it. Denying enemy vessels the use of it forces them to follow longer, more circuitous, and probably more debilitating and costly tracks to their destinations. A strait offering passage through, say, the Lesser Antilles, the loose archipelago that forms the eastern rim of the Caribbean Sea, commands minimal value. There are many alternatives along that arc, most of them easily navigable. Accordingly, none commands exceptional merit in Mahanian terms. Ships could simply bypass contested passages for others just as good.

Contesting the narrow "waist" midway through the Mediterranean Sea, by contrast, can throw a major kink into enemy maritime movement. British reinforcements and transports took to rounding the Cape of Good Hope, at Africa's southern tip, to reach the Eastern Mediterranean during 1942–43, when Axis surface forces and land-based aircraft dealt out hammer blows against convoys transiting the confined seaway separating Sardinia and Sicily from the northern tip of Tunisia.[50] The ability to close the Strait of Gibraltar and Suez Canal would be more potent still—empowering a force to imprison hostile shipping within the Mediterranean or deny entry to foes approaching from the Atlantic Ocean or Red Sea.

Underwater topography and hydrography, then, are crucial to understanding and exploiting the three-dimensional common. Mahanian analysis has a vertical dimension even though he concerned himself mainly with surface shipping. (Mahan perished in the early months of World War I and Corbett shortly after the war, before submarine and aerial warfare began fulfilling their true potential. Hence the two writers' relative silence on these critical matters.) Convoluted channels, shallow water, or shoal water help determine a passage's offensive and defensive potential.[51] A hard-to-navigate passage represents an asset to its defender—a bane to opponents unfamiliar with its intricacies and quirks, even apart from the defender's efforts to obstruct transit.

It is worth appending a point to Mahan's analysis: maritime terrain can change, and it can do so either gradually or abruptly.

Watercourses, especially shallow-water passages, may shift during natural disasters or heavy weather. The Arctic Ocean could become a shapeshifting theater should climate change open polar shipping lanes on a more dependable basis. After all, the ice will advance and recede as seasons change, and it will do so at uneven rates. Strategists must be on guard against such changelings lest they premise operations on using waters or passages that have become treacherous or altogether inaccessible.

The Sea as an Environment That Molds How Seafarers and Aviators Think about Their Professions

The sea—like other operating domains—is a shaper of minds. Socrates cautioned that the unexamined life is not worth living.[52] Adm. J. C. Wylie presents a Socratic examination of the relationship between human beings and the battle space. Wylie contends that a domain's physical characteristics imprint themselves on the minds of those who operate there, and thence mold their assumptions about how to execute military enterprises there. Assumptions matter a great deal to human discourse. After all, any effort at logical proof proceeds from axioms that can be neither proved nor disproved within the system. Participants to a debate must accept the premises as self-evident—or not.

They have a hard time making progress if not. Deadlock often results when debaters operate from incompatible premises. They find scant common ground for dialogue. In effect, Wylie adapts and codifies an old adage familiar from bureaucratic feuds: *where you stand depends on where you sit*. His martial version holds that *where you stand depends on where you operate*. He partitions military folk into different schools of thought, contending that "nearly all practicing strategists" are "either conscious or unaware devotees" of one of four theories, namely, "the continental, the maritime, and the air theories, and the Mao theory of the 'wars of national liberation.'"[53]

Admiral Wylie maintains that ground warriors assume decisive battle is a prerequisite for applying pressure on an enemy's national life, that aviators assume they can control events on the ground by destroying things from aloft, and that seafarers assume command of the sea represents the key to military success. Wylie exhorts mariners to recognize the assumptions and prejudices that stem from their operating domain, and to make allowances for entrenched precepts during debates in joint and allied circles. Wylie urges military practitioners to work toward a shared vocabulary and set of assumptions—thus laying common ground and bolstering prospects for fruitful debates and strategy making.

What Is Sea Power?

Clearly, then, the sea is far more than a vast body of liquid. As noted at the outset, Alfred Thayer Mahan espouses a maritime strategy meant to secure commercial, diplomatic, and military access to trading regions such as East Asia and Western Europe. Were he alive today he would doubtless add South Asia and the Middle East to his list of noteworthy sites. Indeed, he evidently coined the phrase *Middle East*.[54] Prosecuted to good effect, a strategy aimed at access sets in train a virtuous cycle: the navy safeguards access, helping foreign commerce thrive, and commerce in turn yields the tax revenue needed for the upkeep of a great navy. It is the job of statesmen and commanders to perpetuate this cycle into the indefinite future. Only thus can the nation reap the gains from seaward endeavors.

Mahan proceeds to define sea power in more concrete terms, and to consider which societies have the right stuff to do business in great waters. While he was ardently pro-British, he praises a Frenchman, Jean-Baptiste Colbert, for building a foundry for sea power. Colbert acted as secretary of state for the navy during the reign of Louis XIV, the French monarch better known as the Sun King. Colbert learned about maritime affairs from Cardinal Richelieu, the clergyman-statesman hailed as the founder of the French navy. When King Louis granted Colbert a royal appointment in the 1660s, writes Mahan, the navy secretary set about forging "the three links in the chain of sea power," namely, production, naval and merchant shipping, and foreign colonies and markets—"in a word, sea power."[55] This is his classic definition.

Wielders of sea power seek out commercial access alongside other goals handed down by policymakers. Mahan thus depicts industry at home, naval and commercial fleets, and bases and markets abroad as three interlocking components of sea power. And so they are. Commerce, ships, and bases give us our shorthand for elucidating the basics of sea power throughout this volume. Mahan does not put it this way, but sea power must be a product of multiplication of his three variables, not addition. Think about it. If any element of sea power is zero, a people that aspires to sea power enjoys meager prospects. If a country's economy is impoverished, its government has little need for merchantmen and minimal means to fund a navy to protect commerce. Nor does it need foreign marketplaces or naval stations since domestic producers have little to sell and scant need for overseas access.

This may exaggerate—but only slightly. Hypothetically a vibrant industrial power *might* get by with sparse naval or mercantile fleets. It could manufacture goods at home and sell them abroad. But if its government declined to invest in merchant and naval hulls, the leadership would have entrusted the nation's economic fortunes to the uncertain goodwill of foreign competitors that did invest wisely. Wares would have to travel in foreign bottoms, and the government would have little recourse should a hostile navy close the common to trade. Omitting any link from the sea-power chain, then, risks forfeiting national welfare.

If communications—the capacity to use the sea to transport raw materials, finished goods, and military power—constitutes "the most important single element in strategy, political or military," as Mahan maintains, and if the "eminence of sea power" resides in its ability to control the sea lines of communication, then the power "to insure these communications to one's self, and to interrupt them for an adversary, affects the very root of a nation's vigor."[56] Cutting a coastal state's access to the sea is like sundering the roots of a plant. Industry shrivels and dies without nutrients. An industrial power that surrenders its economic fortunes to prospective antagonists exposes itself to having its root system cut. It qualifies as a partial maritime power at best in Mahanian terms. It consents to be a plaything for others.

Nor can an industrial power without access to foreign markets and harbors accomplish much, even if it somehow manages to raise revenue to operate merchant and naval fleets. Hence the weight Mahan lays on access. He pronounces it both the goal of maritime strategy and the motive force impelling it. And hence the weight he lays on forward naval stations. To estimate an oceangoing state's claim to sea power, then, think of its aggregate capacity as a multiple of its potential to carry on foreign commerce; construct, deploy, and sustain commercial and naval shipping; and attain access to forward harbors and bases. A true maritime power casts all three links comprising the sea-power chain.

Gauging Who Has the Right Stuff: Mahan's "Elements of Sea Power"

Mahan wrote to encourage the United States to make itself a seafaring power of note, and he hoped it would measure up by the standards set by past maritime hegemons such as Great Britain, the Netherlands, and imperial Portugal and Spain. He set out to divine what had made those nations great. His journey through oceanic history uncovered six "elements," or determinants of national character and economic and physical might, that equip societies to take to the sea. (I merge two elements, "extent of territory" and "number of population," into a single demographic determinant.)

Mahan presents his discourse on the elements of sea power at the beginning of his treatise *The Influence of Sea Power upon History, 1660–1783*, arguably the most influential American nonfiction book of the nineteenth century.[57] Sea power starts at home, and it demands not just resources but resolve and grit on the part of the people, their government, and the naval establishment. Otherwise resources that might go to seafaring go to other purposes or stay in the ground. His determinants are geographical position, physical conformation, demographics, national character, and character and policy of government.

Geographical Position

Mahan notes that maritime strategy, unlike strategy for the aerial and ground-warfare domains, functions in wartime and peacetime alike. It has "for its end to found, support, and increase, as well in peace as in war, the sea power of a country."[58] Pursued with vigor, it is a restless, enterprising brand of strategy. Entrepreneurial strategists strive without pause to augment their nation's capacity for commerce, diplomatic endeavors, and naval warfare.

A would-be oceangoing power with secure land frontiers—or no land frontiers at all—is blessed by geography. Security at home frees strategists to apply their energies abroad without forfeiting what matters most: the homeland. Mahan points out that Great Britain had no borders to guard against overland invasion. Its leadership could afford to undertake seaborne exploits with "unity of aim" during its era of naval mastery. By contrast, land defense preoccupied the Netherlands. Dutch rulers had to maintain a large army to defend their independence against outside aggressors, even while they constructed a maritime empire that stretched into the Far East. France had the opposite problem: offense tempted its rulers. French monarchs found themselves "constantly diverted, sometimes wisely and sometimes most foolishly," into offensive campaigns aimed at terrestrial conquest and influence.[59] Sharing land frontiers distracts from maritime pursuits.

Geography also represents a liability if it compels a country to divide its forces to protect multiple coastlines. Great Britain's Royal Navy, observes Mahan, enjoyed freedom of movement all around the British Isles and could concentrate fleets for action at will. France has no such luxury. The Iberian Peninsula juts out into the Atlantic Ocean between the French Atlantic and Mediterranean coasts, with the Strait of Gibraltar—and the British stronghold of Gibraltar—interposed between. Paris might need to "swing" fleets between the Atlantic and Mediterranean, but Britain or some other foe could interdict its movements past Gibraltar and stymie French strategy at sea. Such are the dilemmas confronting any country beset by multiple coasts to defend.

Geography has endowed the United States with friendly neighbors to the north and south and aquatic ramparts in the Atlantic and Pacific. It is not an island like Great Britain, but it comes close—and its natural defenses are far broader than the narrow North Sea and English Channel, which furnish Britain its nautical buffer. On the other hand, the fact that the Canadian landmass lies to the United States' north and Mexico to its south prods American statesmen and commanders into a two-ocean strategy while potentially encumbering maritime movement between the oceans. Geography, in other words, prompts Washington to divide the U.S. Navy between the oceans.

However, shifting ships from coast to coast imposed a colossal challenge before the Panama Canal opened in 1915. Vessels had to round Cape Horn, at the southern tip of South America, coping both with distance and with often fearsome weather. Any survey of Mahan's, Theodore Roosevelt's, or other fin de siècle navalists' writings will show how their geographic plight vexed them. The canal helped, but the U.S. Navy did not fully escape its bicoastal dilemma until 1940, when Congress authorized construction of a two-ocean navy.[60] Today, shutting the canal through a naval blockade or other military action would force American fleets to resume circumnavigating South America, much as the battleship *Oregon* had to do to reach the Caribbean combat theater from its duty station in the Pacific during the Spanish-American War.[61] Or U.S. task forces might take the Arctic route, should climate change open polar waters to navigation for part or all of each year.

Either way, a cunning antagonist could repeal the mobility advantage supplied by the Panama Canal—and make geography an impediment to U.S. maritime strategy in some future war.[62] This danger will remain unless Congress fields a U.S. Navy big and powerful enough to stage a fleet in each ocean that can meet challenges there without help from the other fleet. Whether the Navy meets the two-ocean standard today is an open question.[63]

Seafaring states also benefit from easy access to the sea and from being situated near important sea-lanes. Declares Mahan, if "Nature has so placed a country that it has easy access to the high sea itself, while at the same time it controls one of the great thoroughfares of the world's traffic," that country occupies a fortunate strategic position indeed.[64] Britain occupies such a position. The British Isles adjoin maritime routes connecting the North Sea, and in turn the Baltic Sea, with the broad Atlantic Ocean. Germany and the Netherlands found themselves at a severe disadvantage in past naval wars because their major antagonist lay athwart direct access to the high seas. The Royal Navy merely needed to seal the English Channel and the northern waters separating Scotland from Norway. The Russian Baltic Fleet would likewise encounter trouble exiting the Baltic during a NATO–Russia naval war today.

The United States enjoys easy access to the two oceans, and with sufficient resolve and resources it can make itself dominant over the approaches to Panama. Or look at India. The subcontinent's lengthy coastline would let Indian mariners outflank a blockade, while its southern tip adjoins sea-lanes that literally crisscross the Indian Ocean between various entryways to the region. This adds up to an enviable strategic position. On the other hand, India also shares a land border with an aggressive China—muddling its overall strategic outlook. New Delhi cannot throw its resources into sea power wholesale lest it lose out on dry earth.

On the other hand, consider the plight of China, which finds its access to the western Pacific and Indian Ocean encumbered by two concentric series of islands—the "first island chain" and "second island chain" inhabited by potential foes friendly with the United States.[65] U.S. allies could easily seal off the straits piercing the first island chain. Circumstances compel Beijing to worry about access to waters beyond its immediate environs before it has the luxury of worrying about commercial and military access at the terminus of sea voyages. In other words, China inhabits a uniquely unforgiving strategic position among great powers. Its leadership has to fret about access from the time a ship casts off all lines in Tianjin or Shanghai until the time it moors at its destination.

The naval historian peers back into European maritime history to glimpse the importance of various strategic features. He discerns "a very marked analogy in many respects" between the Mediterranean Sea and Caribbean Sea. This analogy promised to take on new resonance once the Panama Canal opened, giving the Caribbean and Gulf their counterpart to the Strait of Gibraltar or Suez Canal. Artificial modifications to geography can carry enormous strategic consequence. Suez spared vessels based in Western Europe the protracted journey around Cape Horn or the Cape of Good

Hope to reach eastern waters. Similarly, writes Mahan, the Panama Canal converted the Caribbean Sea and Gulf of Mexico into "one of the great highways of the world." The Central American waterway spared Atlantic-based vessels from circumnavigating South America or Africa to reach Pacific or Indian Ocean waters, or vice versa.[66]

To derive insights into strategy in coastal or semi-enclosed expanses, make historical study part of geographic analysis. Location may not be destiny the way it is in real estate, but it matters a great deal. To craft maritime strategy, start by looking at the map.

Physical Conformation

Mahan deems seaports strategically placed along a country's shorelines a crucial ingredient of maritime command. Ports are what supply the country its commercial and military access to the sea. He depicts a country's seaboard as one of its frontiers, employing the strikingly modern term "access" to explore the characteristics of maritime borderlands.

While commercial, political, and military access to far-flung regions constitutes the goal and the engine of maritime strategy, access starts at home. Long coastlines are desirable for any would-be seafaring society, but coastlines verge on worthless if not dotted with harbors providing access from the frontier to what lies beyond—namely, the high seas. The more and better harbors endow a country's shorelines, contends Mahan, the "greater will be the tendency toward intercourse with the rest of the world" across the water's edge.[67] Some seaports perform double duty, playing host both to merchantmen and to men-of-war.

Harbors, then, lower the barriers to entry to the maritime common, along with the barriers to entry from the common to the country's interior. What makes a harbor a good candidate for port infrastructure and basing? First, it must exist. "If a country be imagined having a long seaboard, but entirely without a harbor," says Mahan, then it boasts few prospects for high-seas trade or naval power.[68] Harbors that can be outfitted with piers, dockyards, ammunition dumps, and other trappings are a must. Passing goods across the beach in bulk is impractical, as is refitting a commercial or naval fleet at anchor off-shore. It is possible to create artificial harbors, but only at great expense and opportunity costs. In other words, constructing a manmade port drains resources that might be put to better use elsewhere. Few countries can afford to mount such an effort even if willing.

Second, a good harbor is deep and thus navigable for shipping of all shapes and sizes. Shallow harbors—or harbors whose watercourses are so convoluted that ships must make radical switchbacks to enter or leave port—are inaccessible to large freighters and warships. They are of limited use barring major improvements such as dredging channels that deep-draft vessels can traverse. Such public works could impose opportunity costs of hefty magnitude. Such a haven is better than nothing, but it is not a candidate of choice for maritime strategy.

Third, harbors should be numerous. A country that is a beneficiary of many outlets to the common expedites the flow of goods and raw materials from producers to consumers. Especially valuable are harbors that lie at the mouths of major rivers, collocating access to the sea with waterborne access to the backcountry. New Orleans, Rotterdam, and Shanghai are prime examples of well-situated harbors.

Multiple harbors also diversify the country's strategic portfolio, helping outflank a hostile navy that attempts to mount a blockade. Barricading a single seaport is a relatively simple matter. The enemy simply concentrates all its efforts and resources in one place. If it has to blockade many harbors, however, it must break up its fleet into many squadrons, one apiece to cordon off each harbor. In so doing, the adversary disperses the fleet's combined strength into many smaller, weaker packets. More dispersal means a less strict blockade. The feebler each patrol squadron, the better blockade runners' chances of getting to sea and perhaps assailing the squadron. The rigors of blockade duty tend to render long, distended quarantine lines leaky.

Fourth, a harbor must be defensible. Mahan reminds readers that the Dutch navy stood into the Thames estuary in 1667, towing away or burning much of the Royal Navy battle fleet in its home port. Redcoats invaded the Chesapeake Bay and burned the executive mansion—now known as the White House—in 1814.[69] Letting a harbor's defenses languish poses serious perils.

Lastly, but by no means least, the foremost virtue of a harbor for strategists of Mahanian leanings is its geographic location. Well-furnished harbors situated in close proximity to the sea-lanes stand a marine power in good stead for commercial and naval enterprises. Engineers can improve a harbor's defenses, infrastructure, or logistics, but they cannot teleport it closer to important waters, narrow seas, or coastal sites such as enemy bases. Physical conformation is fixed and immutable on the whole, with a handful of exceptions such as Suez, Panama, and other narrow landmasses that can be artificially modified at reasonable expense.

Location may not be fate, but it is fundamental for candidates for seaports. As noted before, the Panama Canal was Mahan's hobbyhorse. He pitched his analysis in large part to explain why the United States needed forward outposts in the Caribbean and Gulf, closer to the Isthmus of Panama. He found Gulf ports such as Key West, Pensacola, and even New Orleans wanting in this regard. They were too far from Panama to support warships patrolling key junctures to regulate mercantile shipping or fend off threats from imperial navies such as Britain's or Germany's. Furthermore, the Royal Navy held the advantage of position from its Caribbean base of Jamaica, astride sea-lanes connecting the Atlantic with the Isthmus. This would not do. (Chapter 2 returns to the role of geography in strategy.)

Mahan offers other commentary on physical conformation. For instance, if part of a country can be surrounded from the sea, or if it is completely separate from the mainland, it is imperative to field a navy able to command nearby waters. Italy is a peninsula separated into eastern and western strips by a formidable ridge of mountains—exposing north-south travel along the coast to bombardment from the sea.[70] Or to take an even more acute example, imperial Japan was an archipelago reliant on the sea for natural-resource imports, in particular oil and rubber, to fuel economic production. Fracturing the sea-lanes connecting the island state with resource suppliers—or, better yet, sealing off communications among the home islands themselves—would spell doom for the Japanese Empire. That is precisely what the U.S. Pacific Fleet did during World War II. Japan was doomed once its navy could no longer command neighboring waters.

The historian also contends that a country's physical conformation orients its people toward the sea, the land, or both, and thereby stamps itself on their political and strategic culture. And since culture molds how people view the world and their place in it, politics and strategy lie downstream from culture. The physical setting, in other words, indirectly helps govern how a society approaches maritime strategy.[71] Mahan compares fin de siècle America with past seafaring societies and finds cause for both optimism and gloom. Both England and Holland suffered from lackluster natural-resource endowments, he finds. Both nations faced the choice between venturing seaward in search of prosperity and staying home in poverty. The Netherlands' predicament was worse: "if England was drawn to the sea, Holland was driven to it; without the sea England languished, but Holland died."[72]

Necessity thus turned both societies seaward and ultimately, by the seventeenth century, pitted them against each other in a contest for maritime supremacy. England prevailed, owing in large measure to its geographic position astride the sea-lanes connecting Dutch shipping to the Netherlands' overseas empire. Both sides went to sea, concluded Mahan, and he hoped his United States would follow suit. But the republic faced a danger: its natural resources were *too* abundant! It would neither atrophy nor die if it turned its attentions and energies inward to North America and neglected maritime affairs. It might even prosper.

In that, America resembled France, a country cursed with "a pleasant land, with a delightful climate, producing within itself more than its people needed." Plying the sea was not a matter of life and death for the French, so rulers could let their attention wander to the detriment of commercial and military seafaring. And, indeed, France constructed a dominant fleet during the reign of Sun King Louis XIV, only to see the navy atrophy when the royal gaze turned to landward conquest. North America's physical conformation presented U.S. leaders and ordinary citizens the option of being landlubbers—and Mahan feared they would exercise it. Resources are a mixed blessing. Natural wealth deprived Americans of a compelling incentive to take to the sea.[73]

Glance around the world again. During the War of 1812 the Royal Navy staged a blockade of New England that suffocated American sea power. Both Yankee merchantmen and the U.S. Navy found themselves confined to port.[74] But that was when the United States remained a few states huddled along the Atlantic seaboard, with rudimentary roads and internal infrastructure at best for shipping goods within the republic. Coastwise shipping carried goods between the states. A stringent blockade thus hampered both external *and* internal commerce.

The United States had spread across the continent by 1890, when the western frontier officially closed. It had developed its harbors and built roads and railways to network production and distribution nodes. From then on it bordered on impossible for even the strongest foe to blockade North America.

China, on the other hand, remains vulnerable to blockades for reasons noted before. It touts coastal economic hubs aplenty, from the Bohai Sea basin in the north to Shanghai and Hong Kong to the south. But the first island chain encloses the entire Chinese coastline. No port outflanks it. Commerce has oriented China toward the sea, yet it faces a potential barricade from occupants of the first island chain. The Indian subcontinent is free of such obstacles, but its long shorelines are almost destitute of viable harbors—which is why New Delhi has taken to manufacturing ports at heavy cost. In short, Mahanian analysis is useful not just for knowing oneself but for estimating the capacity of friends, adversaries, and third parties able to influence the fortunes of U.S. maritime strategy.

Demographics

It seems appropriate to merge two of Mahan's determinants, "extent of territory" and "number of population," into a single demographic index of fitness for sea power. He is referring to the density of the populace relative to the country's square mileage and to the length of its shorelines as well as to the types of skills and aptitudes resident among the populace. Both determinants portray demographics as a basic attribute of sea power. And so it is.

He begins with raw numbers of people relative to the country's physical size, accenting the need for a robust populace. He treats it as a problem of concentration and dispersal, one of the perennial problems in strategy. A sparsely peopled country finds it hard to defend itself against seaborne aggression. The American Civil War, in which he served on blockade duty, represents his example of choice. Writes Mahan, "had the South had a people as numerous as it was warlike, and a navy commensurate to its other resources as a sea power, the great extent of its sea-coast and its numerous inlets would have been elements of great strength."[75]

Yet Confederates were too few in number to shield their ports and inlets effectively against the Union Navy. Nor did they possess the manpower, ships, or armaments to mass somewhere along the Southern coast to puncture the flimsy Union blockade. The Confederacy ultimately lost control not just of its seacoast but of its internal waterways. Union gunboats cruised the Mississippi and its tributaries insolently, slicing the rebellion apart from within. Southerners congratulated themselves on their warlike ethos, but no martial culture could make up for a populace too small to defend its territory.

Mahan also accentuates the types of subgroups that comprise the populace, paying special attention to industries relating to the sea. He confides that not just raw numbers of people "but the number following the sea, or at least readily available for employment on ship-board and for the creation of naval material . . . must be counted."[76] And technological ingenuity is a must in today's ultramodern age. Fielding superior armaments confers tactical and operational superiority if not supremacy. Better technology can also offset inferior numbers, to a degree. Not just shipwrights and aviation builders but a critical mass of software developers, cyberwarfare experts, and other disciplines not related directly to the sea are pivotal for maritime strategy. One imagines Mahan would agree.

A country boasting greater population, consequently, could nonetheless find itself outmatched at sea by a less populous competitor with greater numbers occupied in relevant trades. Eighteenth-century France, to name one such contender, exhausted its maritime manpower in wars against Great Britain despite its larger total population. Britain featured a corps of seafaring expertise that landbound France could not match. After all, the French had to maintain a large standing army while the British got by with a compact imperial force.

Adroit leadership also helped the British tap their fount of national expertise. Mahan relates the story of how sea captain Sir Edward Pellew assembled a frigate crew at the outbreak of war with Revolutionary France in 1793. Seasoned recruits were scarce, so Pellew sought out Cornish miners for his crew. He reasoned "from the conditions and dangers of their calling . . . that they would quickly fit into the demands of sea life."[77] And so they did. After just a few weeks of training, his miner-sailors more than held their own in a duel against a French vessel handled by an experienced crew. In fact, Pellew's tars captured the first enemy frigate taken by the Royal Navy in the war.

Demographics, then, is not always an ally of seafaring peoples. Societies such as Mahan's America are not especially warlike. They resist fielding large standing forces in peacetime and thus stand little chance of scoring quick battlefield triumphs at the outbreak of war. Mahan counsels peace-loving contenders to maintain enough military power in being in peacetime to hold the line when fighting erupts. Postponing defeat buys time to build up strength to compete on equal terms and eventually win, provided they have enough latent strength—including reserve manpower for the navy, merchant marine, and shipbuilding industries—to convert into usable naval might within a reasonable span of time.

Such was the predicament confronting the United States following the December 7, 1941, Japanese naval air raid on Pearl Harbor. Congress had authorized construction of a two-ocean navy in 1940, but shipyards needed until 1943 to turn out combatants and merchantmen in large numbers. After that, new units had to train and then find their way into battle theaters in the Pacific and Atlantic. Rather than crouch down passively in the interim, U.S. Pacific Fleet commanders under-took hit-and-run carrier raids of their own, employing the remains of the Pearl Harbor fleet. They also sent forth sub-marines into the western Pacific to start inflicting damage on Japan's navy and merchant marine until the new fleet arrived in the theater to put steel behind a strategic offensive.

With an economy roughly ten times the size of Japan's—and thus vastly greater military potential—the United States played for time to transform potential into kinetic military power. The U.S. Navy made time its ally despite grievous early reverses. The ghost of Alfred Thayer Mahan is smiling down from heaven.

In short, societies fit for sea power enjoy major reserves of material and human capital to tap. Mahan beseeched the United States to maintain a large merchant marine—"a large com-merce under her own flag," as he put it—in order to groom a corps of seamen for naval service in wartime.[78] This repre-sented an act of cultural upkeep and a way for the United States to make itself resilient—offsetting the demographic shortcom-ings he bemoaned.

National Character

True to his vision of sea power as a mainly commercial under-taking, Mahan accentuates the central part economics plays in sea power. It is no accident, one suspects, that the psalm declares that seafarers "occupy their *business* in great waters" (Ps. 107:23; my emphasis). As this book points out time and again, economic gain is at once the chief aim of maritime strat-egy and its prime mover. Peoples put to sea in search of gain, and their labors yield wealth to fund a diplomatic establish-ment and navy to protect the search for gain. And on and on the cycle goes, if prudently managed.

Mahan proclaims that the propensity to manufacture at home and trade abroad impels peoples to the sea, as does—in the cases of the Netherlands and Great Britain during the age of sail—a poverty of natural resources at home. In fact, he pronounces an enterprising nature a people's main credential for success at sea: "The tendency to trade, involving of necessity the production of something to trade with, is the national characteristic most important to the development of sea power."[79]

A nation suited to sea power thus exhibits a saltwater culture centered mainly on commerce. Martial excellence is a desirable but subsidiary trait. Commerce reigns supreme for Mahan in political and strategic culture, as in maritime strategy. Love of material gain—he borders on saying "greed"—in turn lies at the root of seafaring culture: "If sea power be really based upon a peaceful and extensive commerce, aptitude for commercial pursuits must be a distinguishing feature of the nations that have at one time or another been great upon the sea. . . . All men seek gain and, more or less, love money."[80]

He hastens to add that ingenuity is part of commerce: *how* societies transact commerce is crucial. Some fare worse than others. "Fierce avarice," he maintains, gripped the Spanish and Portuguese empires. They sought not "new fields of industry" in newly discovered regions such as the East and West Indies, Brazil, and Mexico, nor even "the healthy excitement of exploration and adventure." Instead they lusted after "gold and silver."[81] Rather than nurture production and shipbuilding at home, and thus create the lineaments for economic well-being, the Iberian empires extracted natural resources from the Indies while increasingly entrusting their carrying trade to others. Britain and Holland made themselves into nations of shopkeepers, nurtured the entrepreneurial spirit, and performed far better.[82]

Mahan's diagnosis of European maritime cultures is bracing in part because it is politically incorrect. In all seafaring countries, he contends, "social sentiment, the outcome of national characteristics, had a marked influence upon the national attitude toward trade."[83] Societies that held mercantile pursuits in contempt displayed little "national genius" for sea power.[84] Those that honored wealth and the tradesmen who dared much to obtain it tended to flourish. Nobles in Spain, Portugal, and France had scorned trade since the Middle Ages. Elite attitudes begat social disincentives discouraging such lowly endeavors. English and Dutch society celebrated trade, awarding social incentives to the venturesome—those who incurred risk to become rich.[85] In short, cultures that reward enterprise get more of it. Cultures that disparage it get less—and suffer the consequences of self-defeating behavior in the economic realm.

Planting colonies overseas to foster trade is another aspect of national genius for Mahan. Such outposts furnish their mother country with "outlets for the home products and [a] nursery for commerce and shipping."[86] If commercial, diplomatic, and military access to foreign markets represents the summit of maritime strategic success, then founding colonies ruled from home seems like the surest way to guarantee it. Taking control of a territory and governing it is more straightforward than negotiating access with local rulers—and thereby subjecting one's commercial and military fortunes to the vagaries of host-nation politics.

That being said, it is important to note that Mahan is no cheerleader for colonial rule. To be sure, he designates "colonies" as a pillar of sea power. But while he admits to being "an imperialist because [he is] not isolationist," he is not prescribing wholesale territorial conquest of the sort European empires and Japan practiced during his lifetime.[87] He waffles on this point, offering lukewarm praise for the British model while castigating imperialists for succumbing to "entirely selfish" motives for founding colonies. Any colony soon comes to be "a cow to be milked," to be "cared for . . . chiefly as a piece of property valued for the returns it gave."[88] The welfare of inhabitants of the periphery ends up being a matter of indifference for political leaders at the imperial center.

Nor did Mahan exhort the United States to follow the European or Japanese pathway to empire. While he acknowledges that "colonies attached to the mother-country afford . . . the surest means of supporting abroad the sea power of a country," he also insists that "such colonies the United States has not and is not likely to have." Such forbearance has strategic drawbacks. With "no foreign establishments, either colonial or military, the ships of war of the United States, in war, will be like land birds, unable to fly far from their own shores." Accordingly, one of the "first duties" of a maritime-minded U.S. government is to search out "resting-places for them, where they can coal and repair."[89]

Happily, Mahan envisaged little prospect—and little apparent need—for a full-blown U.S. colonial empire to underwrite American sea power. From an early date, for instance, he voiced qualms about U.S. annexation of the Philippine Islands in the wake of the Spanish-American War, when America flirted with European-style empire.[90] If he was an imperialist, he was a diffident one. The U.S. Navy and merchant fleet craved access to foreign seaports—it was the terminal link in the naval "supply chain"—but he appeared agnostic about how diplomats and naval officers should go about obtaining it.

It is commonplace nowadays to bewail American society's indifference to the sea—the citizenry's supposed "sea blindness."[91] The workings of maritime commerce are largely invisible to everyman during daily life, as are dangers to the sea-lanes from nonstate and state malefactors alike. Sea blindness is not some purely American failing. Though decisive, claims Mahan, British sea power was invisible even to Napoleon: "Those far distant, storm-beaten ships, upon which the Grand Army never looked, stood between it and the dominion of the world."[92]

Nor does the U.S. Navy occupy a prominent place in the popular consciousness outside a few coastal hubs like Norfolk or San Diego, where fleets form part of the everyday landscape.

If indeed sea blindness afflicts the populace and its elected leaders, renovating the national character is an urgent project.

Character and Policy of Government

Admiral Mahan compiles a manual of sorts for the types of policies that governments ought to enact to foster the growth and health of sea power.[93] He divides his guidance into peacetime and wartime phases. In peacetime the government can "favor the natural growth of a people's industries and its tendencies to seek adventure and gain by way of the sea," or it can try to midwife maritime industry and culture where they do not exist. Above all, officialdom must recognize that its efforts are capable of "making or marring the sea power of the country," including its commercial and naval components.[94]

In wartime the government can shape sea power by "maintaining an armed navy" commensurate in size and capability with the size of the merchant fleet it is meant to defend as well as the national interests it is charged with upholding. "More important even than the size of the navy" are administrative institutions that favor "a healthful spirit and activity" in the service while helping amass "an adequate reserve of men and of ships" to help the force regenerate combat power after it absorbs enemy punches—as it will in the course of things. Also important in wartime is maintaining naval stations in theaters where the navy must go to protect merchantmen. The navy can either defend its bases itself or, preferably, establish footholds in countries "with a surrounding friendly population" and relieve itself of the burden of defending them.[95]

So much for the generic tasks facing officialdom. Mahan contemplates how the nature of the ruling regime bears on these tasks. The "conduct of the government"—meaning the laws and policies it enacts and the institutions whereby it works its will—"corresponds to the exercise of the intelligent will-power, which, according as it is wise, energetic and persevering, or the reverse," fosters or hinders the development of commerce, ships, and bases.[96] Constancy constitutes his chief concern. What type of regime, he wonders, is most likely to frame and pursue wise, consistent policy toward nautical affairs?

The historian essays some comparative politics to unearth lessons for the seawater-minded America he hoped to see take shape in the twentieth century. He investigates sixteenth- and seventeenth-century European history once again to see how authoritarian regimes perform at building up and husbanding sea power as opposed to more liberal regimes: "Free governments have sometimes fallen short, while on the other hand despotic power, wielded with judgment and consistency, has created at times a great sea commerce and a brilliant navy with greater directness than can be reached by the slower processes of a free people. The difficulty in the latter case is to insure perseverance after the death of a particular despot."[97]

He thus considers autocratic rule first. As noted before, the seventeenth-century French navy was a bequest from Cardinal Richelieu brought to fruition by navy secretary Colbert. According to Mahan, the Sun King's reign witnessed "a most astonishing manifestation of the work which can be done by absolute government ably and systematically wielded."[98]

Colbert, writes Mahan, pursued his aims "in the systematic, centralizing French way." His stewardship of the navy constituted an example of "pure, absolute, uncontrolled power gathering up into its hands all the reins for the guidance of a nation's course." The secretary's "wise and provident administration" saw him apply his energy to forging each link in the chain that constitutes sea power. During his tenure he not only boosted the number of armed ships making up the French navy from 30 to 196, he also reformed naval dockyards to make them "vastly more efficient than the English."[99] Such feats endeared him to Mahan.

Yet royal France illustrates the drawbacks of autocratic rule as well as its advantages. Purposefulness, speed, and directness are virtues of an autocratic order intent on going to sea. Declares Mahan, accumulating the makings of sea power is "simpler and easier" when orchestrated by one statesman, "sketched out by a kind of logical process, than when slowly wrought by conflicting interests in a more complex government."[100]

Still, the hazards of authoritarian rule are stubborn and timeless. Unconstrained by popular or legislative opinion, the authoritarian's mind may wander to landward pursuits. And, indeed, the reform spirit whipped up by Colbert prevailed only until he lost royal favor. His project "withered away like Jonah's gourd when the government's favor was withdrawn" amid the clangor of land war against the Netherlands.[101] Or the autocrat may remain constant, but the autocrat's successor may not share enthusiasm for the seaborne cause. Inconstant naval policy lurks when everything depends on the wishes—or whimsy—of a single despot.

The Netherlands fell under both republican and authoritarian rule during the age of sail. Neither served Dutch sea power well. Mahan depicts the Dutch Republic as a "commercial aristocracy" in which commercial interests "penetrated the government," making it "averse to war, and to the expenditures which are necessary in preparing for war." He upbraids the republic for tightfistedness. Not until "danger stared them in the face" were Dutch officials "willing to pay for their defenses."[102] Naval expenditures detracted from profitmaking.

The republic subsequently withered, giving way to de facto monarchical rule under the House of Orange. Under authoritarian government, the navy suffered from neglect relative to the army, which absorbed national resources for campaigns against the Sun King's France. Mahan's verdict is that the fall of Dutch sea power stemmed from "inferior size and numbers," "faulty policy on the part of the two governments," and the sleepless malice of an external foe, Louis XIV.[103]

While hardly worshipful, Mahan holds up England as the gold standard for sea power. British culture and policy amplified each other in the maritime cause. Wise rulers govern in tune with the prevailing national culture if that culture is oriented toward marine exploits: "A government in full accord with the natural bias of its people would most successfully advance its growth in every respect; and, in the matter of sea power, the most brilliant successes have followed where there has been intelligent direction by a government fully imbued with the spirit of the people and conscious of its true general bent. Such a government is most certainly secured when the will of the people, or of their best natural exponents, has some large share in making it."[104] Government policy toward commerce and naval warfare exerts a galvanic effect on the larger society, rallying the populace for seaborne undertakings. It makes for steady, consistent policy and strategy. Britain was remorseless across the centuries. Mahan applauds British statesmanship on the whole, proclaiming that the "eye of England was steadily fixed on the maintenance of her sea power" at rivals' expense, both in wartime and in peacetime.[105] To name just one example, London deployed diplomacy to quash a nascent Danish East India Company that stood poised to infringe on England's monopoly on seagoing trade.

Imperial German vice admiral Wolfgang Wegener, who served with the High Seas Fleet vanquished during World War I, likewise testifies to the seafaring character of the British government and people. The prewar Anglo-German naval arms race summoned forth an indefatigable response from Britons, observes Wegener, because they "have the sea in their veins owing to their centuries-long [naval] tradition; and [sea strategy] has been instinctively ingrained in their senses, just as we have absorbed the traditions of land warfare."[106] The German navy, by contrast, "remained intellectually a coastal navy" despite its impressive battle line and tactical proficiency, "as the lost war showed."[107] Culture matters—and policy can reinforce culture and be reinforced by it.

Opportunism also numbered among English virtues. The Crown was fortunate in its rivals during England's maritime ascent. European capitals, reports Mahan, "seemed blind to the dangers to be feared from her sea growth." Perhaps because fleets—unlike conquering armies—do their work mostly out of sight, continental Europeans did little to stifle the rise of an "overwhelming power" fated to be used as "selfishly" and "aggressively" as French or Spanish power had ever been, if not quite so cruelly.[108]

In the main, then, the British leadership acquitted itself well by Mahan's peacetime and wartime standards for administration. He does reprimand London for the series of mistakes that led it to undertake a land war in the American colonies, across the Atlantic Ocean, thereby making enemies of the colonists at the same time that dangers were gathering in Europe. Traditional naval policy saw Parliament and the Crown oversee Royal Navy fleet design. London generally strove to maintain a fleet equal in numbers and capability to the Royal Navy's next two biggest rivals combined—the two generally being France and Spain.

Both antagonists were ruled by the Bourbon dynasty and thus were inclined to join forces in war. That handed London a convenient benchmark for naval adequacy. Allowing fleet size to slip beneath the two-power standard wrongfooted the Royal Navy for the American War of Independence, when the French, Spanish, and Dutch navies dueled Britain's navy on battlegrounds from the Virginia Capes to the Indian Ocean. Mahan concludes that the American debacle resulted not from staying true to traditional British policy but from disregarding it. The exception proved the rule.[109]

Similarly, as Admiral Wegener notes, generations of British leaders remained on the lookout for territorial acquisitions that would expand the empire and improve its strategic position. Efficient naval administration, mostly free of corruption, allowed British leaders to transmute natural resources into fleets and supporting infrastructure with minimal waste. And while writers have long lambasted British society for its class consciousness, Mahan points out that the Royal Navy embraced a merit system for promotions through the ranks. Every generation of admirals had some lowborn officers in its midst.[110] The government and naval service harnessed human as well as material resources deftly compared to Britain's continental adversaries.

Mahan closes his account of British performance in the age of sail with a cautionary note about the perils of popular rule. He feared Great Britain might suffer a downfall similar to the Dutch Republic's as the twentieth century dawned. "Since 1815," he laments, "and especially in our own day, the government of England has passed very much more into the hands of the people at large. Whether her sea power will suffer therefrom remains to be seen." While the fundamentals of British sea power still appeared sound, it was unclear whether "a democratic government will have the foresight, the keen sensitiveness to national position and credit, the willingness to insure its prosperity by adequate outpouring of money in times of peace, all which are necessary for military preparation."[111]

While pronouncing judgment on British sea power, he was doubtless aiming this parting criticism at his own country by proxy: "Popular governments are not generally favorable to military expenditure, however necessary, and there are signs that England tends to drop behind."[112] America, he believed, should emulate Great Britain's grand past while heeding the portents of its uncertain future.

• • •

These, then, are the elements of sea power. The first three of Mahan's determinants refer to a country's intrinsic physical qualities; the last three to its human characteristics. The former are immutable, more or less, while the latter are amenable to human action. It is worth asking whether contemporary America retains its national genius for seaborne ventures. Even though foreign commerce is booming, the U.S. merchant marine is in decay. The bulk of American-made goods are transported to overseas markets in foreign-flagged hulls, as are imports arriving in U.S. seaports. Nor, to all appearances, does the U.S. Navy command enough support in Congress to maintain a fleet large and capable enough to discharge all missions assigned it in peacetime and wartime.

The central link in the Mahanian sea-power chain—ships—thus shows signs of fatigue. If American sea power now falls short, it is incumbent on the leadership and everyday Americans to undertake a cultural renaissance that restores sea power to its rightful place in foreign policy and strategy.

Chapter 2 | # How to Keep the Virtuous Cycle Turning

I t is eerie how often human minds run on parallel tracks. As chapter 1 shows, Alfred Thayer Mahan saluted French navy secretary Jean-Baptiste Colbert, a scion of Cardinal Richelieu's realpolitik school of statecraft, for hammering out "the three links in the chain of sea power"—namely, production, naval and merchant shipping, and foreign colonies and markets—"in a word, sea power."[1] In *The Influence of Sea Power upon History, 1660–1783*, Mahan extrapolates from Colbert's labors to a general definition of sea power—a definition centered on trade and commerce.[2] Modern practitioners and scholars see things in similar terms.

In the spirit of Mahan, U.S. Navy outreach accentuates the physical, demographic, and economic characteristics of seaborne enterprises alongside their obvious martial dimension. Strategic wisdom starts with surveying the surroundings. Taking stock of the setting reveals that there is far more to oceanic endeavors than armed strife. Declared Master Chief Petty Officer of the Navy Rick West in 2012: "When I think of the Navy's future I go by the 70, 80, 90 percent rule. Seventy percent of the earth's surface is water, 80 percent of people live near the water, and 90 percent of all trade comes across the water." That being the case, the U.S. Navy must "be out there forward deployed, keeping trade moving and sea lanes open."[3]

And there is no gainsaying Master Chief West's words. The earth is a blue planet, most of its inhabitants cluster along shorelines, and raw materials and finished goods travel predominantly by sea. A ship remains the most economical conveyance for transporting bulk goods, and there seems to be little prospect that aircraft, railways, or trucks will oust fleets of merchantmen from that status any time soon. Navy spokesmen are correct to spotlight the economic and commercial dimensions of seaborne endeavors. Mahan would approve.

And he would add texture to the Navy's message. By "production" Mahan means agricultural and industrial sectors that yield goods for sale on the market. Production also refers to the development of internal communications—roads, railways, canals—that facilitate the transport of goods from a country's interior to trading hubs along its coasts. By "shipping" Mahan means not only ships that carry goods across the sea but also administrative functions and national regulations and laws—notably tariffs—that favor trade. By "colonies and markets" he means foreign markets where finished goods can be sold and raw materials procured to supply manufacturing industries at home. If production, shipping, and colonies comprise three links in a chain, with shipping connecting the domestic economy to external marketplaces, then a country enjoys doubtful prospects at sea unless it forges all three.

Mahan's three links of production, shipping, and colonies and markets have twenty-first-century analogues. While colonies ruled by distant colonial authorities are relics of the imperial past, Mahan would instantly comprehend the logic of today's global markets. The postwar financial and trade architecture rests on the principle of market openness. Multilateral institutions such as the World Trade Organization ensure liberal access to markets for stakeholders in the U.S.-led international economic order. This commitment to openness remains a crucial ingredient in the mobility of goods and services—mobility that in turn facilitates global trade.

Moreover, the global "supply chain" so essential to globalization mirrors Mahan's ideas about "peaceful commerce and shipping."[4] Companies worldwide have constructed an intricate network of interrelationships to produce and handle goods and services, and to distribute them between international markets. Again, Mahan would have been no stranger to the basic mechanisms composing the modern trading system.

He would draw special attention to the system's geographic dimension. As chapter 1 shows, sea power is predicated on immutable "natural conditions" such as ready access to the high seas, the number and location of deepwater ports, and the length of the seaboard.[5] The supply chain also depends on these prerequisites. Inescapable geophysical factors thus dictate the strategic options available to seafaring nations. Geography may facilitate or fetter, channel or bound their maritime strategies. Not even the most canny policy or strategy can flout geospatial reality.

Fast-forward to the twenty-first century, when economists of geographic leanings likewise invoke the metaphor of a chain, in the form of the phrase "supply chain." Hofstra University professor Jean-Paul Rodrigue, to name one, proclaims that three distinct clusters of economic activity constitute global trade. While Rodrigue says little about furnishing the maritime supply chain with a naval protector, what he calls "the geography of production, distribution, and consumption" can be mapped onto any aspirant to commercially driven Mahanian sea power.[6] The supply chain binds together industrial production at home; distribution from domestic points of departure through air, sea, or land transport networks; and markets overseas whereby consumers procure goods to satisfy their needs and wants.

Mahanian sea power is nothing more than a saltwater global supply chain equipped with its own guardian in the form of a navy. Break any link of the global supply chain or the naval "supply chain" and the entire system goes flying apart. Although Rodrigue concedes that he formed his ideas about the global supply chain without reference to geopolitics, his theory nonetheless transposes the Mahanian concept of commercially driven sea power onto the modern system of global trade.[7] Mahan unearths the essential logic of seagoing trade and commerce even if processes specific to his day—notably, conquest of foreign lands—no longer apply. Hence the timelessness and contemporary appeal of his writings.

To Mahan's and Rodrigue's logic of production, distribution, consumption, and naval protection, this chapter adds the all-important if elusive factor of "strategic will" to the sea. Amassing and maintaining sea power demands a conscious political choice. This is a choice a society must make—and reaffirm time and again—to sustain its seaward project. It demands passion. Opening commercial, diplomatic, and military access to faraway theaters to permit distribution and consumption—the aim of maritime strategy—is hard. Without fiery resolve and grit, natural resources remain unexcavated, goods remain unmanufactured, cargo languishes without being hauled across the oceans, and nothing is sold. Prosperity remains out of reach.

Strategists and statesmen overlook this intangible element of sea power at their peril. Sea power is a cycle, but it is not a self-sustaining cycle. Keeping it going demands prudent statecraft. To limit repetition, I consider commercial seaports, domestic and foreign, as a unit; do the same for naval stations domestic and foreign; and then take merchant and naval fleets in turn. The chapter closes with a few words attesting to the importance of bucking up and directing strategic willpower.

Commercial Seaports at Home and Abroad

"Geoeconomics," defined broadly as the interplay between spatial and economic factors in international relations, exerts a powerful influence on the agenda of any nation that covets sea power.[8] Complex, interlocking trading relationships beckon societies to the seas. Maritime-oriented economies figuratively and literally lean into the seas as citizens and industry crowd seashores. Casting the supply chain, then, applies a catalyst for demographic and socioeconomic upheavals that make a lasting and profound impact on a country's seaward orientation. Maritime trade and commerce also entail strategic implications as statesmen and commanders ponder how to defend the links in the supply chain against offshore enemies.

Capturing the entire chain of production, distribution, and consumption would constitute a gigantic task. Let us concentrate instead on the distribution link, particularly on the part seaports play in the supply chain. After all, ports comprise the interface between producers at home and shippers that deliver goods to foreign marketplaces. Ports also provide the interface between sellers overseas and buyers back home. This link is among the clearest manifestations of sea power and maritime trade. And it makes a useful proxy for gauging production and consumption.

Seaports, then, are central to maritime trade. Ports represent an essential component of distribution, the connective tissue joining goods produced at home with shipping that transports those goods abroad. Ports and the global supply chain to which they are affixed are essential to meeting demand for goods in foreign markets. Goods are overwhelmingly shipped by sea, whether measured by tonnage, by "twenty-foot equivalents" (a unit of measurement based on the volume of a standard multimodal shipping container), or by the goods' value. At the same time such distribution networks and nodes ensure that imported goods can adequately meet domestic needs. The number, capacity, and efficiency of ports thus add up to a useful measure of production, distribution, and consumption.

Ports are engines of production and consumption in their own right. Export-oriented manufacturers have an incentive to position themselves near ports or transportation networks that connect to ports, thereby reducing transportation costs. In turn, industries located in or near port cities lure new workers to the seaside. As the local populace and economy grow, residents with rising disposable incomes fuel new demand for domestic and imported goods. Trade begets wealth, and wealth begets more trade, generating a virtuous cycle of productivity and profit growth. Port systems thus mesh with a country's industrial capacity, financial strength, and demographic patterns.

The number and quality of seaports also indicate whether geographical and other structural factors—Mahan's natural conditions—work on behalf of maritime trade and thus sea power. For Mahan, as shown in chapter 1, proximity to important sea-lanes, the length of the shoreline, the number and quality of harbors, the degree to which the population's well-being depends on the oceans, and other factors intrinsic to a country represent essential elements of sea power. The development and health of a seafaring country's port system depend on these features and in turn sustain its sea power.

China probably presents the best contemporary example of the logic of production, distribution, and consumption in action. Since China opened itself to the global economy starting in the late 1970s, government policy has nurtured coastal economic hubs, especially port cities bunched around the Bohai Rim, the Yangtze River delta, and the Pearl River delta. In accord with Mahan's theory, geography—including long shorelines, plentiful harbors, and access to the high seas—favors intense interactions among commerce, ships, and bases along the Chinese seacoast.[9]

It also spurs China's communist leadership to mount a forward defense at sea to shield these hubs from attack—thus spotlighting the nexus among economic development, trade, and military defense.[10] Geoeconomics constitutes the prime mover impelling China's maritime strategy—as it does for any ambitious sea power.

Military Seaports at Home and Abroad

In effect the global supply chain for goods and raw materials has a military twin. Mahan sees what amounts to a parallel supply chain for naval power. After all, a seagoing state needs specialized industry to design, manufacture, and maintain a navy; warships set forth across the same sea-lanes plied by merchantmen; and warships need seaport access on the far ends of their voyages to regenerate their fighting strength. In effect, Mahan takes the global commercial supply chain and pairs it with a defender funded out of the tariff proceeds from commercial transactions.

On the mercantile side, seaports connect domestic producers with merchantmen plying the sea-lanes, and merchantmen put into foreign seaports that connect the goods they have hauled across the sea to foreign buyers. This equates to Rodrigue's cycle of production, distribution, and consumption. In the military counterpart, naval stations at home act as havens to refit, repair, and resupply naval vessels—keeping them not just seaworthy but battleworthy. Some elements of the twin supply chains coincide. In all likelihood, for instance, a country's roster of naval stations is a subset of its commercial ports. Not every commercial port is home to naval forces, but virtually all naval ports double as commercial ports, outfitted with container terminals and infrastructure of all types necessary to move goods and service merchantmen.

From home port, naval task forces venture out to sea to guard the sea-lanes from predators such as pirates or weapons traffickers, or from navies bent on disrupting shipping. Warships benefit from naval stations at the far end of their journeys. In fact, port access is a must. Also helpful are intermediate stops along their way. Bases on foreign soil seldom furnish infrastructure such as drydocks to execute major overhauls, but they can provide most services and stores short of depot maintenance. This is doubly true of hubs where U.S. Navy forces are permanently forward deployed, notably Sasebo and Yokosuka in Japan and Manama in Bahrain. In essence, these are U.S. home ports in foreign lands.

Naval bases, then, are mundane yet indispensable to high-seas operations. A century ago Rear Adm. Bradley Fiske likened their function to "supplying and replenishing the stored-up energy required for naval operations."[11] Like a battery, a fleet's at-sea endurance is far from infinite. Vessels start discharging their stored-up energy as soon as they cast off all lines. It is exceedingly difficult to replenish this energy—manifest in fuel, stores, spares, and ammunition—over vast distances. Even nuclear-powered aircraft carriers refuel every few days as a matter of routine. The ship can steam on indefinitely, but its air wing cannot fly without aviation fuel—and without an operational air wing, a carrier more or less ceases to be a fighting ship.

Nor is refueling and rearming at sea a panacea. The U.S. Navy has raised underway replenishment of fuel, ammunition, and stores to a high art. Asked to list the crucial determinants of Japan's defeat in the Pacific war, wartime prime minister Hideki Tōjō listed U.S. atomic bombs, submarine warfare—and underway replenishment.[12] Underway replenishment liberated battle fleets from port calls for the most part, letting them wage war without pause. The Imperial Japanese Navy never got a breather.

Such testimonials aside, the combat logistics vessels that deliver supplies must themselves be replenished—and often. Explains Fiske, consequently, underway replenishment obviates a navy's need for shore stations only in part. The remaining reasons for bases endure, "especially the reasons connected with machinery repairs."[13] Combatant ships feature modest welding, pipefitting, and machine shops. Submarine and destroyer tenders are specialized ships outfitted to conduct deeper maintenance and repairs, but these workhorse vessels are mainly a thing of the past.[14] Only shore depots can execute full-scale overhauls of U.S. Navy surface vessels—hence the protracted refits ships undergo every few years as part of their operational rhythm.

Admiral Fiske's physics simile conveys the idea that fleets swiftly discharge their potential energy at sea, expending fuel, ammunition, spare parts, and stores. They must put into port to recharge "batteries"—much as travelers plug portable electronic devices into USB ports on long trips to recharge their power supplies. Military seaports represent the naval counterpart to the USB port.

Evaluating Candidates for Military Seaports: Look at Your Map

Where should naval bases be founded? Geography is inescapable. Not for nothing did Franklin Roosevelt urge Americans to "look at your map" during his famous fireside chat on George Washington's birthday in 1942. President Roosevelt was attempting to mold Americans' geographic consciousness and thereby alert them to the dangers posed by Axis legions rampaging across Eurasia and the Pacific.[15] Mortal danger loomed should German, Italian, and Japanese armies join forces. The Axis would surround and strangle the Allies one by one—hence the imperative to marshal all of America's resources to fight.

Look at your map remains a sound starting point for pondering strategic affairs. But beware of consulting maps that convey false or distorted images of reality, as any map—a portrayal of a sphere on a flat surface—inevitably does to one degree or another. Yale professor Nicholas Spykman, one of the giants of geopolitics, opens his masterful short book *The Geography of the Peace* by exploring different projections and considering the impressions they impart.[16] One of Spykman's main messages: *caveat emptor.* Let the buyer beware.

A cautionary aside, then. Cartography educates, but it can also distort or outright lie—with tactical, operational, or even strategic repercussions. Emeritus Fletcher School of Law and Diplomacy professor Alan Henrikson delves into the psychology of geospatial perceptions. He writes that a "mental map" is "an ordered but continually adapting structure of the mind . . . by reference to which a person acquires, codes, stores, recalls, reorganizes, and applies, in thought or action, information about his or her large-scale geographic environment."[17] In that sense, he says, a map is an "idea."[18] Such a map is "'triggered' when a person makes a spatial decision," confronting "a problem that obliges him or her to choose among alternative movements in space."[19]

FDR hoped to adjust Americans' mental map to instill the conviction that they were part of a North Atlantic community that must resist Nazi aggression and that they must regain their standing in the Pacific Ocean following the strike on Pearl Harbor. Henrikson adds that the scale of mental maps varies from person to person. In fact, people often form multiple mental maps of their surroundings. A mental map of the local area may "nest" within the map of the state, country, region, or globe.[20] Or if a particular individual or group harbors stronger loyalties to the local area, it may be that the local map takes precedence over regional or global images. For example, Gen. Robert E. Lee set loyalty to his home state of Virginia above the Union at the outset of the American Civil War—suggesting that his mental map was local in orientation. Otherwise Lee may not have resigned his U.S. Army commission and cast his lot with the Confederacy.

Mental cartography also comprises part of national cultures. For instance, Indian foreign policy commentator C. Raja Mohan explains that Indians entertain a three-layered image of world events. Their innermost mental map spans the Indian subcontinent, the middle map extends across the Indian Ocean region, and the outermost map enfolds the globe.[21] Similarly, contemporary China's mental map centers on

East Asia, riveting attention on the offshore island chain that appears to block access to the western Pacific for Chinese ships and planes.[22] Mental imagery predisposes Beijing to think about foreign policy and strategy in ominous terms. Chinese strategists tend to assign local affairs precedence over regional and global affairs. Their mental maps of the "Indo-Pacific" and the world may overlay their map of East Asia, but ships and planes cannot reach that wider world without attending to access close to home. The Chinese have to think locally in order to act globally.

Nor are mental maps solely about local, regional, or national affinities. People from the same place who operate in different geospatial domains oftentimes see the world quite differently. As noted in chapter 1, Adm. J. C. Wylie explains quarrels among soldiers, airmen, and seamen in part as a function of the domains where they operate.[23] Mental maps of the operating environment give rise to different assumptions about the surroundings and how to conduct affairs there. Or, as Henrikson intimates, the "landsman's view" and "seaman's view" of the world differ from the "airman's view."[24]

The former vantage points lie on the earth's surface—a mostly two-dimensional realm—while aviators think in three dimensions as they soar through the airspace above. Submariners operate in three dimensions as well—and thus may share the airman's view to some degree, despite the disparities between the atmosphere and the undersea realm. Furthermore, Henrikson might have taken a more granular view, differentiating more starkly between the mariner's view and the landlubber's. After all, sea and shore are distinct domains with different properties. When plotting strategy it is worth asking how fellow seafarers, joint-service comrades, and allies, adversaries, and bystanders see the world in geospatial terms. Thinking in spatial terms illuminates. And it aids empathy.

Spykman and Henrikson would also advise strategists to remember that maps can misshape perceptions. As noted above,

Spykman reviews various projections of the earth's surface and observes that they all falsify reality to one extent or another. Henrikson urges the geographically minded to think of everyday examples of how mental maps diverge from concrete reality.

Suppose a commuter is weighing two alternative routes to work. One is a straight-line route from origin to destination, but it takes local roads through congested urban terrain. The other follows an interstate highway on a roundabout route through the countryside, detouring around built-up areas with their traffic and stoplights. It may be that each route takes the same amount of driving time even though one covers far more mileage. One itinerary is shorter and slower; the other, faster but farther. In all likelihood, however, the motorist will picture the alternatives as equidistant. Time shapes perceptions of distance even though the odometer puts the lie to the resulting mental map.

Take one recent and highly influential instance in which mental maps misled. In 2011 Secretary of State Hillary Clinton unveiled the Obama administration's "pivot" to Asia, meaning the U.S. military would "rebalance"—or, rather, unbalance—its force deployments to favor the Pacific theater. The administration codified the pivot in defense strategic guidance in 2012, depicting it as a necessary counterweight to the rise of China . . . whereupon foreign policy commentators instantly took to insisting that America was turning its back on Europe![25]

Mercator maps deceived them, as Spykman might have forecast. Mercator projections commonly situate the Americas near the center of the map, partitioning Eurasia so that Western Europe resides at the far right with East Asia at the far left. From that vantage it indeed appears that Washington must swivel its policy gaze 180 degrees to look from London or Paris toward Tokyo or Beijing. To avoid such misperceptions Spykman beseeches international relations practitioners to look at things from multiple standpoints before drawing strong conclusions about policy or strategy.

Looking down on the North Pole from space, as a polar-centered azimuthal equidistant map does, makes it plain that U.S. forces based on the East Coast sweep around one side of Eurasia when bound for the Indian Ocean.[26] They usually pass through the Atlantic Ocean, Mediterranean Sea, and Red Sea along their way. Forces stationed on the West Coast or at Hawaii cruise around the other side of Eurasia to reach the western Pacific. Visually, a polar projection makes it appear as though the world island is enjoying a comforting American embrace.

I used to close a lecture about the pivot with a slide featuring Spykman's polar map. I festooned the map with vectors illustrating U.S. military movements, and I closed out the talk by declaring that "Eurasia Is for Hugging." Washington need not take its eyes off Europe to concentrate on Asia. U.S. policymakers merely deflect their gaze a few degrees southward to the Mediterranean Sea, along the sea route skirting Europe's southern ramparts. This presents—or should present—small cause for alarm. U.S. leaders may have come to regard Europe more as a platform for endeavors in the Indo-Pacific than an object in its own right, but that is a far cry from deserting the continent. An old book explains "how to lie with statistics," or rather how to avoid being lied to by them.[27] *The Geography of the Peace* proffers similar counsel in the realm of cartography. Take it.

Through such observations Nicholas Spykman shows how geography pervades strategy. Some sea-power experts add geography to the Mahanian formula as a fourth element alongside production, ships, and bases. I do not. Geography stands apart from and above these other factors. It sets the arena where these elements of sea power interact, and its contours are fixed for the most part. This is why Admiral Mahan and like-minded strategists regard acquainting oneself with the geographic surroundings as a prerequisite for success in competitive enterprises. Such scrutiny acclimates commanders and officials to the field where they will compete or do battle—and alerts them to which possibilities terrain opens and which it forecloses.

Small wonder that Mahan proclaims "geography underlies strategy."[28] He expresses his ideas about strategic geography most fully when investigating potential sites for U.S. naval bases. While maritime geography differs vividly from continental geography in many respects, he observes that some principles of terrestrial warfare apply at sea. Consequently, the feats of land-power giants like Frederick the Great and Napoleon Bonaparte represent a worthy object of study even for mariners. Mahan delights in quoting or paraphrasing Napoleon's maxim that "war is a business of positions," doing so four times in *Naval Strategy* (1911), his last major work—a work specifically meant to reveal the likenesses between land and sea warfare.

Why did Mahan carry principles of land combat out to sea? Simple: he was the son of West Point professor Dennis Hart Mahan, a revered figure among U.S. Army officers to this day.[29] The younger Mahan imbibed ideas shaping ground combat from one of the masters from a tender age. And he remained acutely conscious of geography throughout his lifetime. After all, terrain dictates how practitioners of ground warfare ply their trade to a degree that seafarers and aviators find hard to fathom. Soldiers think in terms of mountains and hills, defiles and elevations. Mariners find their way across the open ocean using polar coordinates, mathematical instruments and formulas, and, nowadays, satellite navigation. Aviators do much the same in the wild blue except they maneuver in three dimensions rather than on the level plane that is the sea. As chapter 1 points out, only close to land does maritime or aerial movement come to resemble movement on dry earth.

In light of his land-warfare upbringing, Mahan examined specific theaters more exhaustively than did the other greats of maritime theory. He was an acolyte of Antoine-Henri Jomini, a land-power scribe he christened his "best military friend."[30]

Indeed, some commentators pronounce Mahan a seafaring Baron Jomini.[31] Jomini served with Napoleon's army, and he laid great weight on the geometric aspects of land warfare. His writings inspired such influential concepts as lines of communication and interior and exterior lines.[32] Lines of communication map nicely to the oceans, which lend themselves to straight-line courses except at the origin and terminus of a voyage, or when a vessel must pass close to land to go through a strait or cruise along the coast.

Both Prussian sage Carl von Clausewitz and Chinese general Sun Tzu, to name other legendary figures in the strategic canon, likewise pay tribute to terrain in a generic way. Neither surveys the geographic characteristics of any particular battleground or theater in any detail. Mahan does because he has an agenda. In his lifetime he fretted about how America could make itself an oceangoing power of consequence, so he aimed his findings and recommendations about strategy chiefly at the American government and society of the late nineteenth and early twentieth centuries. He implored Americans to turn their attention and competitive energies to regions he deemed critical. He delved into specifics about those regions.

While the term "rimlands" had not yet been coined—Spykman fashioned it in the 1940s—the historian thought constantly about access to coastal Eurasia. Rimlands are intermediate zones between the sea and the deep continental interior. Mahan paid special attention to the Far Eastern seaboard, yet his findings apply to any aspirant roughly comparable to the United States or to Great Britain, America's forerunner as ruler of the seas.[33] U.S. steamships needed regular supplies of fuel and stores to reach important theaters. Thus, commercial and naval fleets needed "stepping-stones" across the Pacific Ocean along with dependable access to dockyards on the far end.[34]

Failing to obtain outposts would relegate U.S. fleets to the status of "land birds, unable to fly far from their own shores."[35]

They would accomplish little if confined to home waters. The beneficent cycle of production, distribution, and consumption would never get started let alone churn into the distant future. This would not do. Naval stations are no luxury for maritime strategy. If radiating sea power far from home was tough, Mahan insisted the United States seek bases along likely routes to the rimlands to boost the fleet's range. Mahan started with the necessity to carry on trade in the Far East and worked backward from the western Pacific to figure out where prime spots for naval stations lay.

His attention alighted first on the Hawaiian Islands, then on the Isthmus of Panama, and finally on the Caribbean Sea basin. He was writing before the Spanish-American War. The 1899 peace accord delivered Caribbean islands, Guam, and the Philippine Islands into American hands.[36] Having acquired Midway Island in 1867, Congress now annexed Pacific redoubts such as Hawaii and Wake Island—fabricating an island empire from next to nothing almost overnight.[37] Steamships now enjoyed logistic support on journeys to the Asian rimlands as part of the spoils of armed conflict against Spain.

Mahan's writings had long faced southward. It is worth pointing out that he was well ahead of his time in thinking about new nautical passageways and facilities needed to support and defend mercantile shipping making its way through them. Not until 1902 did the United States conclude a treaty empowering Washington to dig and fortify a canal across the isthmus.[38] By then Mahan had already been compiling his brief for forward U.S. outposts for almost two decades. It often takes time for practical politics and strategy to catch up with abstract strategic designs.

As befits a veteran of Union Navy blockade duty against the Confederacy, Mahan started surveying strategic geography with a short treatise on *The Gulf and Inland Waters* (1883), a history of naval operations in southern waters during the Civil

War. The book helped earn him a faculty post at the Naval War College in 1886. In *The Gulf and Inland Waters* he appraised the geopolitical worth of ports such as New Orleans, Mobile, and Pensacola, hinting at the direction his thinking would later take.[39] Mahan thus commenced exploring strategic geography seven years before his masterwork, *The Influence of Sea Power upon History, 1660–1783*, appeared in 1890 and over three decades before the Panama Canal opened for business in 1915.

As noted earlier, Mahan charted the new sea route to Asia in phases, starting with the goal—steppingstones across the Pacific Ocean—and working his way back toward points of departure along the U.S. East Coast. He started clamoring to annex the Hawaiian Islands by 1893, when he published an essay titled "Hawaii and Our Future Sea Power" in *The Forum*. He then traced the nascent route from the Pacific back to the Isthmus of Panama (in the article "The Isthmus and Sea Power," published in the *Atlantic* later in 1893), the "gateway" between the oceans, and thence into the Gulf of Mexico and Caribbean Sea (in "The Strategic Features of the Gulf of Mexico and the Caribbean Sea," published in *Harper's* in 1897). He thus sketched the sea-lanes that would constitute the distribution link in the supply chains for commerce and naval power.

All three essays were reprinted in *The Interest of America in Sea Power* in 1897. The timing of publication can have been no accident. War with Spain was looming that year, and with it, opportunity beckoned for the United States to expel a European empire from nearby waters and make itself master of the Caribbean basin. Backers of empire needed intellectual support for their cause, and Mahan helped supply it at a critical juncture. As Theodore Roosevelt might have said, the political "kaleidoscope" turned. Political conditions aligned so that partisans of maritime imperialism could win over Congress and put their Mahanian design into effect.[40]

Hawaiian Islands

Mahan thus took maritime strategy in phases. The Caribbean and Gulf would become America's entryway to the Pacific once the canal opened, offering direct passage to Hawaii and thence to the Far East. Why Hawaii? The archipelago's geostrategic value explains why. It is the closest island steppingstone to the North American West Coast, and it is the only candidate around. It thus commands peerless value. He points out that "the Hawaiian group possesses unique importance—not from its intrinsic commercial value, but from its favorable position for maritime and military control."[41] To arrive at this verdict the historian formulates three indices for estimating the value of candidate sites for naval stations:

> The military or strategic value of a naval position depends upon its situation, upon its strength, and upon its resources. Of the three, the first is of most consequence, because it results from the nature of things; whereas the two latter, when deficient, can be supplied artificially, in whole or in part. Fortifications remedy the weaknesses of a position, foresight accumulates beforehand the resources which nature does not yield on the spot; but it is not within the power of man to change the geographical situation of a point which lies outside the limit of strategic effect.[42]

This is one of the most powerful passages in Mahan's massive body of work. By "situation" he means a potential hub's geographic position. If situated near important seaways, enemy bases, or other places commanding strategic value, then it is well situated by Mahanian metrics. If not, its value ranges from so-so to negligible. "Strength" refers to a site's defensibility. Natural defenses are ideal, but navies and armies can "harden" a site by digging in, constructing rugged buildings and shelters for aircraft and ships, or emplacing armaments around it capable of striking against hostile forces offshore or aloft. "Resources" means the port city's and adjacent countryside's capacity to support the fleet with food, fuel, and stores. If a site's resource endowment is slender, it must be augmented by erecting logistics infrastructure adequate for bringing in supplies.

Proximity to important sites or sea-lanes is supreme while isolation detracts from a harbor's value. For example, Gibraltar overshadows access to the Mediterranean Sea. But it would be worthless as a naval station, despite its unsurpassed natural defenses, if repositioned to waters devoid of merchant and naval traffic—say, to the empty middle Atlantic.[43] A fleet based there would find little to do. Hostile shipping would bypass it. Nor, as Mahan notes, would anyone see any point in attacking the harbor. Stout defenses would be moot. Nor can a sea power do much to improve an isolated feature's location. Natural defenses can be supplemented, or resources can be shipped in overland or oversea. Position is eternal.

Mahan appends a fourth metric to his analytical score sheet alongside position, strength, and resources—namely, the social, cultural, and political context in countries that consent to host naval bases. He notes in passing that "a certain regard must be had to political conditions, which may be said to a great extent to neutralize some positions." Social or political dysfunction can degrade a site's value or nullify it altogether. Mahan discounted Haiti as a U.S. base for just that reason. The island's constant revolutionary upheaval, or sociopolitical "nothingness," reduced it to "an inert obstacle" rather than an asset to U.S. maritime strategy.[44] Access was undependable at best.

Mahan's comments about the politics of host nations sound like an afterthought, but he does confirm that position, strength, and resources are not everything. Learning the local human terrain can be just as crucial. After all—thankfully—strong nations no longer wrest choice pieces of territory from their sovereigns to build bases. Seafarers must take account of prospective host nations' interests, views, and woes or risk seeing access to their bases curtailed or refused in stressful times.

If the leadership disregards the human terrain a conflicted or incompetent host government could set the strategic value of a prized site at naught. U.S.-Philippine relations are a modern example of troublesome relations with a former colony and current defense ally. Manila asked the U.S. military to leave the archipelago after Mount Pinatubo erupted and demolished U.S. facilities there in 1992. Sentiment among many Philippine residents and elites favors an American return to the islands in hopes of curbing Chinese abuses in the South China Sea. Yet inviting a former colonial master back is anathema to major segments of popular opinion. The uneven human terrain for U.S. basing would not surprise Mahan.

Hawaii stacks up ideally by the Mahanian index of geographic position. Mahan pays homage to "the first Napoleon," who made a habit of surveying the terrain first when "commenting upon a region likely to be the scene of war."[45] Bonaparte would take stock by

considering the most conspicuous natural features, and then [enumerating] the commanding positions, their distances from each other, the relative directions, or, as the sea phrase is, their "bearings," and the particular facilities each offers for operations of war. This furnishes . . . a clear estimate of the decisive points. . . . The number of such points varies greatly, according to the character of the region. In a mountainous, broken country they may be very many; whereas in a plain devoid of natural obstacles there may be few, or none save those created by man. If few, the value of each is necessarily greater than if many; and *if there be but one, its importance is not only unique, but extreme*—measured only by the size of the field over which its unshared influence extends (my emphasis).[46]

The Hawaiian archipelago would have captivated Napoleon. It lies 2,400 miles southwest of San Francisco, at the center of a circle devoid of alternative way stations where shipping could tarry. The islands stand astride important sea-lanes, including tracks connecting the Panama Canal with East Asia. In British imperial days the route linking western Canada to Australia also played a critical part in maritime strategy.[47] Hawaii lies along that route as well. Indeed, the U.S. Navy and Marine Corps fought in the Solomon Islands in 1942–43 in large part because Adm. Ernest King, the chief naval overseer of the Pacific War, feared the Imperial Japanese Navy would sever the shipping lanes that connected North America with Australia via Honolulu. In short, the archipelago commands extreme value in Mahanian parlance—making the effort to equip, fortify, and supply Pearl Harbor worth the trouble and expense.

Central America

The Isthmus of Panama would become a crucial node for shipping en route to Hawaii and thence to Asia. Mahan christened the canal the "gateway to the Pacific for the United States." It lent his strategy for southern waters its overarching purpose.[48] For him, everything centered on building a canal across Panama (or perhaps Nicaragua) and deploying a battle fleet to safeguard its approaches against predatory empires. Mahan reminded sea-power enthusiasts that the isthmus had been a thriving portal for overland transshipment of goods between Atlantic and Pacific—and thus "a point of general interest to mankind"— for centuries before engineers conceived of digging an artificial waterway between the oceans. He contended that "enterprising commercial countries," because of "the very characteristics which make them what they are . . . are led perforce to desire, and to aim at, control of these decisive regions. . . . Consequently, in every age . . . there will be found manifested this desire for control; sometimes latent in an attitude of simple watchfulness; sometimes starting into vivid action under the impulse of national jealousies, and issuing in diplomatic rivalries or hostile encounter."[49] The lust for gain drew attention to places on the map that expedited trade.

Such was the isthmus' lot. Declares Mahan, the "decadent military kingdom of Spain" depended on treasure from Mexico and Peru and tribute from the Philippine Islands, which had "flowed towards and accumulated around the Isthmus." Great Britain relied on the Caribbean basin for trade and commerce during its wars in the Western Hemisphere and beyond. So dependent was it that, in 1779, King George III vowed to keep a Royal Navy fleet on station in the Indies even if doing so exposed the British Isles—the homeland—to invasion.[50] For Mahan it was an iron law of international relations that nations found their "surest prosperity" through control of such seaways and thus would compete with one another to control them: "Where factors of such decisive influence in European politics were at stake, it was inevitable that the rival nations, in peace as well as in open war, should carry their ambitions to the scene; and the unceasing struggle for the mastery would fluctuate with the control of the waters, which, *as in all maritime regions*, must depend mainly on naval preponderance, but also in part upon *possession of those determining positions*, of whose tenure Napoleon said that 'war is a business of positions.' Among these the Isthmus was chief" (my emphasis).[51]

The desire for economic prosperity riveted the great powers' attention on the isthmus. Its importance derived from such permanent factors and was part of "the natural order of things." And, he declared, "control of the Central American Isthmus means naval control, naval predominance, to which tenure of the land is at best a convenient incident." Mahan concluded that the United States held the "predominant interest" on the isthmus because of its two-ocean geography, which inhibited "rapid and secure communication between our two great seaboards." Thus, "our interest is both commercial and political, that of other states almost wholly commercial. . . . no settlement can be considered to constitute an equilibrium, much less a finality, which does not effect our preponderating influence, and at the same time insure the natural rights of other peoples."[52] Unsurprisingly, then, Mahan put the United States first. The logic he espoused for America's "Mediterranean," or middle sea, holds for any aspiring sea power that possesses the economic vitality, military strength, and political resolve to make use of important strategic features.[53] Molding events on and around the Isthmus of Panama preoccupied not just Mahan but like-minded navalists such as President Theodore Roosevelt and Sen. Henry Cabot Lodge—statesmen positioned to put Mahanian ideas about saltwater affairs into effect.[54]

Nor were they the only Americans to feel the canal's cultural and political tug. Contends Nicholas Spykman, making that "cut through Central America"—amending geography through human ingenuity and drive—wrought a turnabout in American strategic and political culture. The United States naturally faced eastward toward Europe owing to its heritage as an offshoot of the British Empire and a destination for European immigration. Yet Spykman insists that constructing a new channel between the oceans swiveled "the whole of the United States around on its axis."[55] A republic that had inclined eastward since its founding now gazed first southward to its Mediterranean, then westward toward the Pacific Ocean.

If trade and commerce are the beating heart of maritime strategy, the Panama Canal had sweeping practical import. In effect, the transoceanic shortcut teleported New York closer to the Pacific Ocean and the riches that American business interests expected to find there. Merchantmen based in New York now had a shorter journey to Shanghai than did British competitors based in the major commercial seaport of Liverpool. Modifying geography granted American shippers an instant competitive edge. No longer did they have to round a continent to pass from one ocean to another. And voyages between North American coasts were now shorter by thousands of miles, easing internal communications within the United States.[56]

Caribbean Sea and Gulf of Mexico

Defense of this precious asset posed a problem. Mahan worried that European navies would build naval bases in the Caribbean and Gulf in hopes of regulating the flow of shipping to and from the isthmus—possibly at the expense of the U.S. interests he held dear. He found that prospect unbearable and implored the U.S. Navy to find sites for its own bases to take charge of the situation. But where? Mahan sketched the sea-lanes through southern waters and singled out Jamaica and Cuba as compelling candidates for forward outposts. When rating the islands' merits, he pronounced Jamaica prime real estate: it "flanks all lines of communications."[57] Judged purely by its situation, the British-held island commanded the greatest potential of any site in the Caribbean Sea. On the other hand, it was deficient by the standard of resources. It depended on freight brought in by sea from Canada or the British Isles to sustain the fleet. Thus, this compact island was vulnerable to a naval blockade.

And Cuba? The island overshadowed Jamaica. Mahan deemed Cuba a miniature continent that adjoined all sea routes stretching from the Atlantic Ocean to the British bastion. In other words, a hostile fleet stationed there—presumably an American fleet—could isolate Jamaica in times of strife and slowly starve it out. Great Britain would have to allocate a dominant navy to Jamaica to imbue the island with its full strategic value. By the age of Mahan, however, it appeared increasingly doubtful that the Royal Navy could outmatch the U.S. Navy in the U.S. Navy's home waters.

In fact, the Royal Navy more or less vacated American waters by the turn of the twentieth century. London bowed to U.S. Navy preeminence while taking solace in Washington's relative goodwill. Or as historian Samuel Flagg Bemis puts it, British leaders "rather definitively acquiesced in the predominance of the United States in that part of the world."[58] And strategic priorities warranted a pullout. London needed to summon home squadrons to face down imperial Germany, which had commenced bolting together a battleship fleet in the North Sea.

American suzerainty made a withdrawal possible, and the Anglo-American marriage of convenience more or less nullified Jamaica as a threat. That left Cuba. Cuba was virtually self-sufficient in terms of resources and natural defenses—and retained its value even if a stronger fleet were not stationed there.[59] It represented Mahan's site of choice for a forward base to oversee the waters connecting the isthmus to the Atlantic. Florida harbors such as Pensacola and Key West were wanting. They lay too far away. In resource terms, they were remote from the rest of the country. Many sites—for instance, Pensacola; Mobile Bay, Alabama; and New Orleans—lay close to one another on the map. Some were "overshadowed by others so near and so strong as practically to embrace them."[60]

Guantanamo Bay, Cuba, was another matter. Because Cuba was a large, elongated island abounding with navigable harbors and natural resources, forces could resupply themselves while moving from side to side in the interior to outmaneuver and defy blockading squadrons.[61] The miniature continent measured up by Mahan's three standards—position, strength, resources—while it was hard to say whether the islanders' politics would be a problem should Spanish rule be ousted. Host-nation relations thus constituted a neutral factor in the Mahanian calculus. After tallying up the advantages and drawbacks of the candidates, Mahan urged the U.S. Navy to ensconce itself in Cuba—making itself the heavyweight force in America's middle sea.

What should we take from this foray into nautical geography? First, land and sea are interdependent. The capacity to use the sea as an offshore sanctuary bestows the capacity to project influence ashore, where great affairs of state are decided. At the same time seagoing forces need bases on land in order to refresh crews and hulls to operate at sea. There is a symbiosis between water and dry land.

Second, there exists a law of supply and demand in strategic geography. If islands or coastal sites are well located and few in number, they take on strategic worth even if their resources, their natural defenses, or the conformation of their harbors disappoint. The scarcer the supply of geographic positions, the heavier the demand for them. Still, evaluating the merits of rival contenders for naval stations remains crucial before the government makes the political, financial, and military investment in obtaining, improving, and protecting a base. Otherwise finite public resources may go to waste.

And third, it is worth pointing out that technology is reshaping the interplay between sea and shore. We inhabit an age of land-based sea power. Any implement able to shape events at sea is an implement of sea power. It need not be a ship-launched munition or tactical aircraft. Long-range precision strike weaponry backed by advanced sensors and other surveillance technology can radiate force from land far out to sea. Unmanned aerial, surface, and subsurface vehicles play a mounting part in naval warfare. Cyberwarfare could disrupt a foe's networks or sensors, isolating formations or individual units from one another and subjecting them to attacks that defeat them one by one. The permutations for combining and recombining instruments of sea power appear virtually limitless.

Chapter 3 says much more about the symbiosis between the fleet and shore-based fire support. For now it suffices to note that sea power is no longer an exclusive province of battle fleets or even of navies. Air forces, armies, nonnaval services such as coast guards, and even not strictly governmental services such as merchant marines or maritime militias can exert influence on the high seas. These are all tools of maritime power. No sound maritime strategy can ignore them—any more than it can ignore basic geographic facts.

Ships: The Merchant Marine

As befits a theorist who sought to make his teachings a possession for all time, Mahan offers few specifics about the size and shape of mercantile fleets. He pitched his works mainly to American audiences since making the United States a serious commercial and naval power constituted his goal. Still, he also meant his works to have value to any aspirant to maritime might. Some countries have nationally owned merchant marines, others rely on private shipping firms for their carrying trade, and others have a mix of public and private shippers. He may have seen little point in delving into details.

He did hammer home a few major points. First, he takes a genuinely *maritime*—as opposed to naval—outlook on the seaborne enterprise. The historian sees freighters as strategic implements and bearers of national greatness as surely as ships of the line that garner honor and renown in close action. He stresses that commerce is the drive shaft of maritime strategy. Merchantmen carry raw materials and finished goods across the sea, embodying the distribution link in the global supply chain. They connect production with consumption, in Jean-Paul Rodrigue's parlance.

Second, commercial vessels should be plentiful in number and not too capacious. Mahan peers back into age-of-sail history to divine why, say, English and Dutch seaborne commerce prospered and endured while Spanish and Portuguese commerce shriveled over time. The main reason, he concludes, is that Iberian empires clumped the carrying trade into a few large hulls while the English and Dutch dispersed theirs among large numbers of smaller merchantmen. Each lumbering Spanish or Portuguese galleon bore a major share of the nation's resources. He thus hints that constructing ships with too great a hauling capacity entails hazards. The search for efficiency inclines shippers to embark cargo in a few hulking vessels—yet that entails strategic peril.

Mahan thus suggests that the economies of scale in the shipping industry could turn out to be false economies when things go wrong on the high seas—as they will sooner or later. Concentrating goods in big packets risks forfeiting a sizable percentage of national wealth should even a single ship be lost to weather, pirates, or commerce raiders. A dispersed commercial fleet is resilient by contrast. It can withstand the loss of a few vessels without undue economic hardship. Each ship represents just a token percentage of the aggregate carrying capacity. Mahan's verdict: "Where the revenues and industries of a country can be concentrated into a few treasure-ships" such as Spanish galleons, "the sinew of war may perhaps be cut by a stroke; but when its wealth is scattered in thousands of going and coming ships, when the roots of the system spread wide and far, and strike deep, it can stand many a cruel shock and lose many a goodly bough without the life being touched."[62] Dispersal, then, confers staying power.

Third, Mahan voices a strong preference for maintaining a national U.S. merchant marine as opposed to surrendering the distribution function to private hands or foreign carriers. As chapter 1 shows, he insisted that a robust merchant fleet ensures that a ready reserve of skilled seamen will be on hand to augment the navy in wartime. It also provides a reserve of hulls that can be quickly converted for military use. Tapping that reserve maritime strength is harder when manpower and ships belong to private firms. Legal impediments intervene. It is harder still when American goods travel in foreign-flagged vessels—as they overwhelmingly do nowadays. Foreign merchantmen and seamen lie beyond the government's legal reach altogether. They do little to supplement sea power or entrench the nation's saltwater culture.

In other words, a vibrant national merchant marine furnishes a "hedge," a stratagem for reducing the demands, rigors, and risks of sea war. Conscripting commercial shipping is common practice during major conflicts. During the world wars, for instance, navies converted ocean liners for use as troopships to ferry soldiers and war matériel across the Atlantic Ocean en masse. Freighters, oilers, and ships of all shapes and sizes joined the merchant marine for the duration. Great Britain's Royal Navy requisitioned the container ship *Atlantic Conveyor* to transport helicopters and other supplies to the South Atlantic during the 1982 Falklands War. The examples go on and on. Merchant sailors and ships perform double duty when nations come to blows. It behooves governments to husband that mundane yet vital implement of sea power.

And, fourth, there remains the question of how to defend merchantmen against nautical predators. Mahan comes at this question obliquely at best. He concedes that commerce raiding, or *guerre de course*, is "doubtless a most important secondary operation of naval war, and is not likely to be abandoned till war itself shall cease." He touts its impact even though he considers it "a delusion, and a most dangerous delusion," to think it wins wars on the high seas.[63] It is not decisive in sea war, yet it can wreak devastation on enemy maritime traffic—as Confederate raiders did to Union fleets during the Civil War.[64] Diversifying the merchant marine reduces the repercussions of losing a few ships to brigandage or commerce raiders.

To this we might add that the best methods for protecting commercial shipping depend on from whom it needs to be protected. Mahan concerns himself mostly with full-blown sea war, so navies are the foe he has in mind. His recommendations reflect wartime exigencies. Apart from a large fleet, convoys constitute a time-tested solution to the problem of *guerre de course*. Commanders assemble large bodies of merchantmen and assign them armed naval escorts to ward off submarines, surface raiders, and land-based aircraft. For instance, Allied navies fought a Battle of the Atlantic in each world war as the United States sought to ship manpower and war matériel to Europe unmolested. Coupling convoys with land-based patrol aircraft and roving light-carrier task forces provided a solution to the U-boat problem in the second Battle of the Atlantic.

Japan supplies a negative testament to the efficacy of convoys. For reasons that remain somewhat obscure, the Imperial Japanese Navy neglected to institute a convoy system until the summer of 1944, when much of the Japanese merchant fleet was strewn across the Pacific seafloor after falling prey to U.S. submarine warfare.[65] Tokyo's neglect empowered the U.S. Navy to unravel a maritime empire that was bound together only by the goods and natural resources carried from territory to territory in mercantile hulls. Tokyo's oversight nearly proved fatal, allowing the foe to sap Japanese industrial strength. It may have proved actually fatal had the United States foregone dropping atomic bombs on Hiroshima and Nagasaki and opted to blockade and starve out the Japanese home islands.[66]

The question of shipping defense is different in peacetime, when guarding against nonstate scourges is the challenge. For example, pirates imperil sea-lanes in heavily trafficked expanses such as the Gulf of Oman, Gulf of Guinea, and South China Sea. Navies can dispatch warships to patrol them, but these are large bodies of water. Squadrons must spread out to impose adequate geographic coverage. Dispersing opens seams between patrol vessels that brigands can exploit. It also slows down response times as counterpiracy ships make their way to scenes of attack. What to do?

The time-honored European practice was to arm commercial ships to defend themselves. That ensured firepower was on hand at points of impact. Merchantmen could be very heavily armed during the Age of Sail. For example, merchant vessels pressed into royal service made up about two-thirds of the English battle fleet that beat back the Spanish Armada in 1588.[67] These days governments need not go to such extravagant lengths to fend off lightly armed corsairs. Merchantmen can take certain simple precautions against pirate assault. Crews can steer evasive courses, transit troubled sea-lanes at high speed, or remove ladders and other fittings from their ships' sides that make it easy for pirates to board. And, of course, crews can be armed or armed detachments—marines or private security personnel—stationed on board during a run through pirate-infested waters. The principle of self-defense applies across the centuries.

One imagines Mahan would voice dismay at the present state of U.S. merchant shipping. American-flagged vessels are few in number, whereas competitors such as China maintain large inventories of merchantmen and require them to be built to military standards to simplify and expedite the process of converting them for wartime use.[68] Washington should take a lesson from its rivals, from its own past constructing and requisitioning merchantmen during the world wars, and from Mahan as it manages the composition of the U.S. civilian fleet and the strategic sealift it provides.

Ships: The Navy

Alfred Thayer Mahan is less specific about how to constitute naval fleets than many believe. As noted at the beginning of this volume, it is commonplace even for experts to reduce him to his advocacy of armored battleships, point out that battleships are no more, and dismiss him as a relic with little insight into a high-tech missile age. But Mahan wanted his ideas to endure for generations. He understood that technology and war-making methods change, and thus he confines himself to some general pointers able to weather the passage of time.

In reality, Mahan was a proponent of "capital ships," not battleships per se. He defined capital ships not as a specific type of hull or weapons configuration but as "the backbone and real power of any navy." These are "the vessels which, by due proportion of defensive and offensive powers, are capable of taking and giving hard knocks."[69] Capital ships represent the core of a Mahanian battle fleet. They dish out punishment against roughly symmetrical enemy fleets, absorb punishment that comes their way, and fight on to victory.

This definition remains a valuable place to start thinking about how to design a fleet. In his day the battleship indeed stood at the vanguard of naval warfare. Gunnery remained fighting ships' chief weapon until the inception of military aviation a century ago. A battery of big guns guided by effective fire control lent the battlewagon its offensive power. Thick armor, compartmentation (subdividing the hull into watertight compartments so a hit does not flood the entire ship and sink it), and other innate design features lent such heavy hitters their defensive power. Naval architects thus trusted "passive" defenses. Their guiding assumption was that battleships would take a hammering from enemy ships boasting roughly comparable hitting power—and must be built ruggedly enough to withstand it.

Any ship fitted to mete out and take heavy blows can qualify as a capital ship, the premier combatant of its age. Air-power enthusiasts such as Gen. Billy Mitchell started claiming that aviation had superseded battleships as early as the 1920s, when Mitchell oversaw an experiment during which aircraft sank the ex-German battleship *Ostfriesland*. It is customary, however, to designate December 7, 1941, as the date when naval aviation eclipsed surface combatants. That is when Imperial Japanese Navy carrier airmen unleashed air-launched torpedoes and bombs against the U.S. Pacific Fleet battle line to deadly effect. By the end of World War II carrier aircraft had sunk the

Japanese super-dreadnoughts *Musashi* and *Yamato*. Displacing 70,000 tons and bristling with 18.1-inch guns capable of slinging 3,200-pound shells twenty-six miles, these were the largest and most heavily armed dreadnoughts ever built. If they could not stand up to air power, no surface vessel could.

The deaths of *Musashi*, *Yamato*, and countless lesser surface combatants affirmed the supremacy of the aircraft carrier and its striking arm, the embarked air wing. These were vessels that could deal out destruction across hundreds rather than tens of miles. The Mahanian standard, then, can still help us evaluate claimants to capital-ship status and thus can help fleet designers configure navies. It is worth noting, however, that capital ships' defensive power has come to reside more and more in "active" defenses and less in passive defenses such as armor. That is, defenders try to strike down opponents at a distance before they can launch their weapons. And modern vessels' offensive firepower lies not just in aircraft but in the guided missiles that aircraft, surface combatants, and submarines now fire. Thus, missiles provide modern fighting ships much of their offensive *and* defensive power.

What is today's capital ship? Is it still the big-deck aircraft carrier? Perhaps so. Carrier aviation can strike across hundreds of miles. Carrier hulls are built on a philosophy similar to battleships of old. They are sheathed with heavy armor to shield their innards. And not only does the air wing execute an active defense of the fleet, ranging far ahead to smite enemy aircraft and ships before they close to weapons range, but a carrier steams with a retinue of cruisers and destroyers equipped to defend this "high-value unit" against aerial, missile, and subsurface attack. On the other hand, prospective foes such as China have armed themselves with antiship ballistic and cruise missiles, many of which outrange carrier air power and can be launched in volleys. Whether the carrier's defensive power still suffices is one of the most pressing questions confronting seafarers today.

What about fighting ships such as guided-missile cruisers and destroyers? Such vessels abound with offensive power. Mahan's eyes would gleam at their banks of vertical launch cells, each of which can disgorge one or more missiles to pummel an enemy fleet or targets ashore at long distances. That's firepower. On the other hand, naval architects have dispensed with armor almost entirely. No longer are surface combatants built to take a punch from their own main battery and keep fighting, as battleships could. They are dependent on such active defenses as antiship and antiair missiles, electronic jamming, and close-in gunnery meant to stop threats before they can strike the ship.

The goal in current U.S. Navy parlance is to strike down the "archer," a missile-armed enemy unit, before he can launch his "arrow," or missile. If such measures fail, surface combatants' hulls lack the resilience to absorb many arrows. Critics mock "one-hit ships." Mahan would find fault with surface combatants' claim to capital-ship status.

Or could the submarine be the capital ship of the future? Missile-armed attack subs tote the offensive firepower to assail enemy subs or surface fleets at long range. They carry lethal torpedoes. Many are outfitted with vertical launchers capable of lofting a family of antiship missiles at enemy fleets. Subs boast substantial defensive power alongside this offensive power. Their passive strength, however, resides less in stout hulls or active defenses than in stealth. The characteristics of the sea let them evade enemy attacks rather than withstand them. Differentials in temperature, pressure, and salinity allow them to hide from enemy sensors, primarily acoustic sensors such as sonar.

A submarine does not carry the same offensive firepower as a carrier, cruiser, or destroyer, but it commands an inarguable edge in survivability over these vessels through sheer elusiveness. It could stake its claim to capital-ship status. Again, the Mahanian formula for ascertaining which fighting ships represent the fleet's chief striking arm retains its potency a century later. It also helps us judge claims that there will be no standalone capital ship in future combat—claims that "human-machine teaming," unmanned vehicles, cyberwarfare, or some other exotic construct could become the fleet's main repository of offensive and defensive power.[70]

The ghost of Mahan's contemporary Sir Julian Corbett could chime in on the subject of fleet design. He pays less attention to capital ships than does Mahan. Mahan wrote to urge America to assemble a fleet of capital ships where no such fleet had existed before. As a Briton, Corbett saw little need to convince his nation to construct a battle fleet. The Royal Navy already boasted the world's foremost such fleet. Instead he holds forth on fleet design. Corbett surveys the "threefold differentiation" among the ship types that make up the navy as a whole, dividing them into capital ships, "cruisers," and the "flotilla."[71] He refuses to enthrone capital ships at the center of naval warfare. In fact, he designates them as support ships for lesser craft. This is an avowedly counter-Mahanian perspective.

In passing, Corbett speculates that this division of labor is neither fixed nor eternal. Ships are ideas made manifest, he says: "the classes of ships which constitute a fleet are, or ought to be, the expression in material of the strategical and tactical ideas that prevail at any given time."[72] Ship types vary not only with technology but with the concepts in vogue in a particular epoch and country. In other words, ships are cultural artifacts as well as warfighting implements. He leaves unsaid what happens when navies shaped by radically different ideas about strategy, tactics, and ship design collide. Such intellectual and material asymmetries are worth pondering to glimpse the future character of battle.

In Corbett's scheme, as in Mahan's, capital ships comprise a battle fleet that duels hostile battle fleets for control of the sea and the fruits that come with it. (Chapter 3 has much more to say about the phases of naval warfare that Corbett identifies.)

For him, though, capital ships exist not to fight battles for battle's sake but because enemy capital ships may threaten friendly control of the sea-lanes. Lesser warships—cruisers and flotilla craft—exercise that control. These plentiful but lightly armed combatants are too weak to fight off enemy capital ships without help from the fleet. Capital ships exist to furnish that help. The battle fleet, then, is the guardian of smaller craft that fan out across the sea-lanes in large numbers to exercise command. "The true function of the battle-fleet," Corbett maintains, "is to protect cruisers and flotilla at their special work" of policing the sea. "Destroying the enemy's armed forces" remains "the paramount object" of naval warfare, but winning major battles is not a goal in itself.[73] It is merely an enabler for all good things that follow.

Cruisers are lighter and less expensive than their heavyweight brethren. Their chief virtue is that the navy can afford them in bulk, yet they still outgun most of the hostile vessels they can expect to encounter when policing the sea. They scatter out in the maritime common to ensure that friendly forces and merchantmen can traverse it safely and to deny hostile powers the use of the common. Once capital ships wrest command from the enemy, it is safe for cruisers to exercise command. This is cruisers' "special work," as Corbett phrases it. Flotilla craft are lesser craft still. Unarmed or lightly armed, they conduct the administrative tasks all navies must perform, typically in near-shore waters. They too defend on protection from the battle fleet.

In short, finance is a stern taskmaster. No navy enjoys infinite resources for shipbuilding and fleet design. Ascertaining the proportion of the budget and shipbuilding resources that should go to capital ships, cruisers, and the flotilla thus represents one of the most nettlesome challenges before fleet designers. Skimping on capital ships might leave the fleet with firepower too anemic to seize control of important waters from a strong rival. A navy cannot exercise command that it never wins.

Yet an excess of battle capacity entails hazards of its own. Too small a cruiser or flotilla contingent would leave commanders with too few assets to police the common and reap the blessings of maritime supremacy. "In no case can we exercise control by battleships alone," confides Corbett. "Their specialization has rendered them unfit for the work, and has made them too costly ever to be numerous enough. Even, therefore, if our enemy had no battle-fleet we could not make control effective with battleships alone."[74] Allotting too much to capital ships would prove self-defeating if the opportunity cost was the fleet's ability to exercise maritime command.

Again, how to apportion resources is a perennial problem. Let me side with Mahan against Corbett on this question. It is safer to err on the side of a surplus of combat power rather than risk a deficit. It is easier to fabricate or convert light, cheap, relatively unsophisticated warships—Corbett's cruisers and flotilla craft—amid the din of war than try to make up a shortfall of complex capital ships. At the same time Corbett is correct to warn against skewing resources *too* lopsidedly toward high-end combat. Striking the right balance should be fleet designers' aim.

Corbett appends an important caveat to his analysis. In his day, at the onset of the age of steam, new technology was equipping cruisers and even the flotilla with firepower on a scale formerly reserved to capital ships. Smaller vessels increasingly brandished torpedoes and sea mines—armaments capable of doing grievous damage to capital ships. In theory, even short-range craft such as torpedo boats, minelayers, and rudimentary diesel submarines could deny the battle fleet freedom of movement off an enemy's coasts.

The upshot? Rather than concentrate solely on augmenting capital ships' hitting power against peer capital ships, tactical commanders were now forced to fret about screening the battle fleet against flotilla vessels or cruisers, ships heretofore beneath notice. Corbett's lament: "the whole naval art has suffered a revolution beyond all previous experience, and it is possible the old practice is no longer a safe guide." The best strategists could do was glean what they could from history while peering through a glass darkly into the future. Corbett prophesied a "structureless fleet" lacking the well-defined division of labor characteristic of sail-driven navies.[75]

A superempowered flotilla and cruiser force thus turned the world upside down during the days of Corbett and Mahan, and it has remained inverted ever since. If anything, the revolution has progressed even further. Even diminutive craft such as China's Type 022 *Houbei* catamaran or Sweden's *Visby* corvette pack a wallop in the form of antiship missiles—the high-tech descendants of the rudimentary torpedoes that vexed Corbett. Iran's Islamic Revolutionary Guard Corps wrings significant value out of speedboats roaming the cramped waters of the Persian Gulf. A missile fired from a flotilla craft can do as much damage as one disgorged from a cruiser or destroyer. And in this age of long-range precision strike weaponry, the flotilla may not be entirely made up of ships. A shore battery could dispatch missiles scores or hundreds of miles out to sea, lending its own firepower to the fleet. So could a warplane flying from an airfield on shore. So could unmanned craft. This is the essence of "access denial" and "area denial," measures that local defenders increasingly deploy to fend off hostile navies from their shores (chapter 3 reviews the concept of access denial at some length).

Yet there is still value in this approach to fleet design. Corbett's neat division of labor among ship classes may have broken down, but the functions—battle, police duty, administrative work—remain. His fleet taxonomy still offers an enlightening way to think about fleet and ship design even today, a century after technological progress upended the order of things.

So much for fleet *design*; how should fleets be *deployed* to best advantage? Scholars and practitioners have long accused

Mahan of issuing a mandate: "Never divide the fleet!" He never said such a thing. Such a maxim caricatures the far more nuanced advice he offers naval commanders and their political masters.[76] He explains how to size fleets and fleet detachments. A "broad formula," he contends, is that a contingent "must be great enough to take the sea, and to fight, with reasonable chances of success, the largest force likely to be brought against it."[77]

Mahan was not known for parsimony with words, but this succinct passage abounds with insight. Parse his words. The passage brings together the material dimension of sea combat with questions of concentration and dispersal of ships and firepower, management of probability and risk, and geopolitics. First, he compiles a "broad" formula, not some algorithm whereby commanders calculate with scientific precision how many and what types of ship to assign to a particular fleet. War is an interactive clash of wills between antagonists determined to get their way. They deploy ingenuity and resources to overthrow their enemies. The resulting topsy-turvy setting defies exact calculations of friendly and enemy capabilities. Commanders cannot calibrate the fleet's size and strength precisely to the demands it will face. Efficiency is always a concern, but it cannot be their overriding concern.

Second, Mahan says the fleet must be "great enough" to wage a trial of arms. How can commanders judge what makes their fleet great enough relative to foes? Beware of common shorthand for fleet size and power. Overreliance on simple metrics such as tonnage, numbers of hulls, and so forth can distort the picture. Tonnage means only that one fleet outweighs another in terms of displacement, not combat power. The statistic is not meaningless—bigger ships can carry more fuel, weapons, and stores—but tonnage reveals little in itself. Brute numbers of hulls likewise reveal little about a fleet's battle capacity. After all, an aircraft carrier counts as one hull, but so does a winsome patrol boat. There is no trustworthy single proxy for whether a fleet is battleworthy. Thus, there is no substitute for estimating the firepower each fleet can bring to bear at likely scenes of combat, factoring in *all* indices of strength.[78] And even then the guesswork quotient will likely remain substantial. This is a fact of naval warfare.

Third, the fleet must be shaped to match up against the "largest force" it is likely to encounter with "reasonable chances" of success. Mahan reminds commanders that superiority is relative, not absolute. Candor about one's own capabilities and limits is good and praiseworthy, but making a reasonable estimate of enemy capabilities and limits is essential to forecasting the probable balance of strength in a realistic scenario. That means not just comparing the power of each naval fleet but comparing the power of the joint naval, ground, and air force each contestant can bring to bear at a particular place on the nautical chart. This is Mahan's "largest force" at a scene of battle. Such a broad-based view also helps commanders manage risk—Mahan's "reasonable chances"—determining how much they wager by sizing a fleet this way or that.

And fourth, commanders must gauge how powerful a foe they are "likely" to confront. This is not merely a question of measuring physical strength; it is a political and strategic question. At its most basic, strategy is about setting and enforcing priorities. How great a fraction of its forces a combatant risks in a particular theater depends on how much it cherishes its political and strategic goals there, and it depends on what competing commitments it intends to uphold elsewhere on the map. A global power such as the United States today, or Great Britain in its imperial heyday, cannot apply all of its resources to one effort unless it cares so deeply about its objectives there that it is prepared to forfeit other commitments and interests. Few interests warrant such expense and risk. Instead the leadership usually strives to keep as many of its commitments as possible. It subdivides its resources—dedicating a fraction of the total force to defend each commitment.

Estimating the fraction likely to appear in a local adversary's vicinity hands that adversary a yardstick for sizing and shaping its own fleet. The Royal Navy remained at least a hypothetical foe during Mahan's lifetime, but it had a worldwide empire to administer. Unless the Crown or Parliament was prepared to risk Britain's imperial holdings and interests in places like India or Africa, they could not commit the bulk of the Royal Navy to some contingency in, say, the Caribbean Sea. The fragment they would be prepared to commit gave Mahan his measure of U.S. naval adequacy. He calculated that a fleet of twenty battleships would equip the U.S. Navy with sufficient power to fight the British contingent it was likeliest to meet in action while entertaining reasonable prospects of success.

That left the U.S. Navy far inferior to the Royal Navy in overall ship count yet strong enough to make itself locally superior in waters Americans treasured most. That was enough. Mahan affirms that "decisive local superiority at the critical point of action is the chief end of the military art, alike in tactics and strategy."[79] The United States could amass decisive local superiority where it mattered and when it mattered in its maritime environs—achieving its goals at sea without outbuilding the Royal Navy in an open-ended arms race. Washington could settle for global inferiority while making itself locally superior.

This sophisticated approach to strategic calculation is a far cry from "never divide the fleet." Mahan mainly worried that Washington would subdivide the U.S. Navy strategically so that detachments could not render one another mutual support when one ran into trouble in wartime. Creating Atlantic and Pacific fleets, he cautioned, could leave the navy inferior to challengers such as Japan or Germany in both oceans—and could expose both fleets to crushing defeat. Better to leave one coast unguarded and keep a dominant fleet in one ocean than divide up the navy and risk losing it all piecemeal.

This perspective is why Mahan gazed in horror as the Imperial Japanese Navy crushed the Russian Navy by increments during the Russo-Japanese War of 1904–5. Russia broke up its navy among the Baltic Sea, Black Sea, and Pacific Ocean. Japan's Combined Fleet annihilated the main Russian Pacific Fleet in the Yellow Sea in August 1904 (a cruiser squadron based at Vladivostok escaped destruction), then turned around and annihilated the Baltic Fleet in May 1905 after St. Petersburg dispatched that force to the theater to restore Russian naval power. Mahan pointed to Russian handling of the campaign as an example of how not to transact maritime strategy.[80] The stronger antagonist lost out by being strategically imprudent. America's navy must avoid a Russian fate.

It is possible, then, for a local power to impose mastery of its own offshore seas while remaining inferior to a regional or global power. In fact, that is a desirable state of affairs. Such a contender does not invest in excess military power. It husbands national resources while still accomplishing political and strategic goals. Not until World War I did the United States see the need for "a navy second to none." Not until World War II did it construct shipping in such numbers that it could in effect station a self-contained navy superior to likely foes in each ocean. But the U.S. Navy ruled American waters from roughly 1900 onward. It fielded adequate battle capacity without excess capacity.

Strategic Will to the Sea

So much for the process of assembling the rudiments of production, distribution, and consumption and deploying a protector to guarantee the safe turning of the virtuous cycle. National willpower is what sets the sea-power cycle in motion and keeps it going. Strategic will electrifies maritime strategy. It rallies a populace, government, and military, lending a sense of purpose and enthusiasm for the nation's maritime destiny. Resolve imparts direction and momentum to maritime strategy—helping propel the maritime cycle into the indefinite future.

A brief detour into a different conception of sea power is worthwhile. According to Adm. Wolfgang Wegener, a cruiser skipper in the German High Seas Fleet during World War I, sea power is a product of "strategic position," the fleet, and "strategic will" to the sea. Strategic will is the important part for our purposes here. At first blush Wegener seems to demote the human factor, as manifest in strategic willpower or resolve, to secondary status. He contends that "two things . . . beget sea power"—namely, the "fleet and strategic position. Only in conjunction, not separately, can they constitute sea power. Of the two elements of sea power, one—the fleet—is a tactical factor, while the other—strategic position—is a geographical factor."[81]

By "strategic position" Wegener means naval stations sited near important trade routes. From strategically situated bases, warships can control the sea-lanes, ensuring a free flow of exports and imports while denying that freedom to foes in wartime. Commerce is king for him, as for Mahan. Commercial motives apply the catalyst for seafaring states to seek out forward positions, either by conquering them or by negotiating basing rights with host nations. In turn, the fleet is a tactical implement that commanders wield to fight for, win, and exercise control of commerce.

However, Wegener advances the startling claim that geography and the fleet are unconnected to each other. Strategy, he says, relates to land while tactics is about water. "At sea . . . tactics rest with the water and strategy with [the fleet's] geographical position [relative to] the land."[82] He adds that while strategy for ground forces begins at the outbreak of war, "the navy's begins in peacetime, entirely separated from tactics. Consequently, naval strategy is not strictly a military problem but rather a joint problem for soldiers and statesmen in peace and in war."[83]

Because maritime strategy spans the saltwater and terrestrial domains and should animate governments and societies in times of peace and war alike, diplomats and senior commanders must work together to launch the fleet on its quest for strategic position and guide its progress toward that commercial and geographic goal: "If army and navy belong as brothers in arms owing to their joint operations plan in war, then navy and Foreign Office should be twin brothers because in peacetime they must jointly pursue the strategy that augments sea power. The tie that firmly binds foreign politics to the navy is the strategic will to sea power."[84] In short, human sinews—ingenuity, far-sightedness, competitive instinct—bind together the fleet with its geographic goals. Wegener not only designates strategic will as a third factor in his sea-power formula but appears to regard it as the dominant factor. He applies the catchphrase articulated by nineteenth-century German philosopher Friedrich Nietzsche— the "will to power"—to maritime strategy.[85]

Continues Wegener: "World power and sea power, world politics and maritime strategy are unified entities because their purposes and effects flow from the same source, the 'strategic will.' The strategic will is nothing other than the will to power turned toward the sea. A nation that lacks strategic will lacks the will to sea power." The strategic will "operates through the strategic operations plan and guides the tactical fleet to strategic position. *The strategic will breathes life into the fleet*" (my emphasis).[86] Without the will to power, the fleet is a lifeless mass if it is built at all. It wins no battles and does nothing to improve the nation's strategic position. It is inert.

Mahan offers pungent commentary on the importance of national character, deeming it a determinant of sea power. His concept is rather static. Wegener does Mahan one better, showing that national character manifests itself in strategic willpower.

It is more than a mere prerequisite for going to sea. It is a primal force that gives life to the seaward quest and lashes seafarers onward. At the same time, strategic will demands constant nurture from framers and executors of policy and strategy lest the virtuous cycle of maritime trade, commerce, and military power sputter.

This is where imperial Germany fell short. Wegener laments time and again that centuries of continental warfare had imprinted on German minds a distinctive way of thinking about martial affairs—transposing ideas about land combat to the sea and blinding Germans to the importance of strategic position for a maritime empire intent on seagoing trade and power projection. Germany's dearth of seafaring traditions left the fleet and its political masters with little instinct to carry the fight to antagonists such as Great Britain and its Royal Navy. In short, Germans lacked the fire in the belly needed to outcompete established rivals on the high seas.

Rousing and sustaining popular sentiment, then, is central to a country's bid for sea power. Managing the social and cultural dimensions of maritime strategy poses a challenge of the first order for statesmen as well as wielders of the diplomatic, economic, and military instruments. Without competitive fire innate in the populace—kindled, fueled, and tended by people in high places—a society commands meager prospects when embarking on its seaward project. Political and strategic leaders should bear in mind that culture is malleable. It is possible to mold a national identity, fashioning a national narrative that favors seaborne endeavors.[87] Charismatic leaders able to frame maritime strategy in terms of national destiny as well as tangible gain are well placed to rally strategic will to the sea. If they do, the nation may fulfill its maritime strategic aims.

Chapter 3 | What Navies Do

From the makings and rhythms of sea power we now turn to the practical side of how navies further the operational, strategic, and political aims entrusted to them. A force fulfills its mission by doing the things familiar to all mariners, such as drawing up and administering shipbuilding programs and operating and overhauling equipment. Naval leaders must also tend to the human factor in naval warfare. U.S. Air Force colonel John Boyd reminds posterity: people, ideas, and hardware—in that order—are the chief determinants of success and failure in human competition.[1] To invigorate the human factor, the leadership must mold a culture that fits the strategic and operational surroundings and keeps pace as those surroundings change around the service.

As they will. Renaissance Florentine philosopher-statesman Niccolò Machiavelli makes this point forcefully, portraying founding a new state or institution as the most formidable act of statecraft.[2] Adjusting the culture of that state or institution amid fluid times comes next in importance and difficulty—especially if the institution has grown corrupt and needs to be purified. Stasis kills. And yet human beings and their institutions dislike change. They find it an ordeal.[3] Machiavelli contends in effect that nature has hardwired individuals to continue doing what worked in the past until harsh experience compels them to do otherwise. Fortune varies, but they remain set in their ways. Sailors are fond of the old saw "if it ain't broke, don't fix it." The saying conveys an essential Machiavellian truth—that few people reform old ways until reality proves the old ways are "broke," and proves it in unequivocal fashion.

As it is with individuals, so it is with organizations, which after all are bodies made up of individuals to whom philosophers' wisdom applies. Institutions discharge their functions through standard methods, yet the world refuses to stand still to accommodate their preference for routine. This clash between human nature and mercurial surroundings forces leaders to amend standard operating procedures or court disaster. Ruin follows when they fail to break shopworn patterns of thought and deed. Leaders throughout the institutional hierarchy, then, must take charge of their corporate destiny—and undertake constant cultural renovation to thrive.

Strategic Constants

If institutional practices must change to stay abreast of the times, tenets of strategy endure. Maritime strategy is about access, and it is about control. To ensure commercial, diplomatic, and military access to important rimlands such as Western Europe, East Asia, and South Asia, a navy and affiliated joint forces must amass the capacity to control physical space. In particular, they must assert control of the links in the economic geography of production, distribution, and consumption. Transposed onto the map, control starts at home. Maritime forces must shield coastal economic hubs and seaports where goods are loaded aboard ship and take to the sea-lanes. They must regulate the maritime common—the connective tissue connecting producers to consumers—in the interest of safe shipping. They must oversee access to foreign seaports where cargo is unloaded for distribution to buyers.

And they must project an image of power and competence as they do all this. They must impress audiences able to grant or withhold, abridge or deny access to the region. Others may contest access to the common or to harbors overseas. At its most fundamental, in fact, strategic competition is an inter-active contest of wills between competitors determined to frustrate rivals while getting their way. The safest assumption when making strategy is that antagonists are possessed of inge-nuity and passion that equal or excel one's own. These are not inert masses on which maritime strategists work their will. In sports parlance, two wrestlers grappling constantly for strategic advantage make a better metaphor than the lone boxer pound-ing away at a punching bag.[4]

A concept from statesman-scholar Henry Kissinger helps practitioners think through how to succeed in this disorderly setting. Kissinger set out to describe how one nuclear-armed state deters another, but his concept applies in equal measure to conventional deterrence and coercion of foes and to reas-surance of allies and friends to boot. Deterrence is the process of convincing a prospective aggressor not to do something we wish to proscribe. We issue a threat to do something drastic—such as use atomic weaponry—if hostile leaders defy us and try to instill confidence in them that we will inevitably carry out our threat if they do what we forbid. If we make believers of them, and if the action we are threatening would exact a pen-alty or inflict costs they are unwilling to bear, then they should desist by deterrent logic.

Kissinger reduces the confidence-building process to a sim-ple algorithm. "Deterrence," he writes, demands "a combina-tion of power, the will to use it, and the assessment of these by the potential aggressor." He adds an important coda: "deter-rence is a product of those factors and not a sum. If any one of them is zero, deterrence fails."[5] This is basic algebra. Multiply a variable or variables by a tiny fraction and the product of multiplication is very small. Multiply even very large numbers by zero and the product is zero. In other words, all the physical brawn in the world means little if its possessor lacks the resolve to use it. Even overbearing might backed by dauntless will-power means little if the antagonist remains a doubter.

The basic logic of capability, resolve, and belief applies not just to nuclear but to conventional deterrence. Particularly in this era of long-range precision arms, it is possible to threaten to use conventional weaponry to defeat an opponent or to compel that opponent to pay a frightful if not unbearable price to achieve its goals. Furthermore, Kissinger's formula applies not just to deterrence but to coercion. Coercion involves issu-ing a threat to induce an adversary to do something it would otherwise refuse to do (as opposed to convincing an adversary to refrain from doing something it might prefer to do—the goal of deterrence).

And his concept applies to reassurance. Aggregating one's strength with others' only makes sense when trying to face down a domineering antagonist or oversee the vast emptiness of the marine common. Recruiting allies and coalition part-ners is far easier when partners believe in one's capability and steadfastness. Telegraphing power and resolve in a convincing manner makes it politically safe if not appealing for others to enlist in some cause. They need not fear being left in the lurch by inept or vacillating partners. They can join worthwhile endeavors with reasonable hopes of success. In short, Kissinger's formula provides a way to think about missions that navies may discharge, all the way from routine alliance diplomacy through high-end warfare.

The Australian maritime scholar Ken Booth brings this down to the practical level, supplying a prism for refracting what navies do on a daily basis and, thus, a convenient way to explore the profession of arms at sea. To employ the oceans as a medium for moving goods and people, extracting natu-ral resources, and projecting power for diplomatic or military purposes, he writes, seafaring states build navies to execute diplomatic, police, and military functions.[6] This chapter follows Professor Booth's general arrangement, examining these three functions in turn. It makes a detour between the discussions of police and military functions, exploring the "wicked problems" endemic in the "gray zone" between peace and war.

Diplomatic Role

Naval diplomacy comes first among Booth's trio, and it can advance political and strategic aims in a variety of ways. Peacetime strategy for a global maritime power such as the United States is what Carl von Clausewitz would term a strategy of "negative aim." Negative aims are status quo aims.[7] A power prosecuting such a strategy has no desire to take something from others. It merely wants to keep others from taking something away or otherwise undercutting the status quo. In other words, the custodian of an existing order such as the global supply chain sets out to preserve that order—preventing others from corroding or shattering the chain.

Naval diplomacy advances negative aims in peacetime. It's commonplace within the U.S. military establishment to list diplomatic, informational, military, and economic instruments of national power—the ubiquitous DIME—in that order. Doing so implies all four instruments are coequal. I dissent. Diplomacy stands above the other instruments and choreographs their use for strategic and political gain. Diplomacy is negotiation, after all. What purpose do tools of national power serve if not to strengthen the hand of national leaders when they negotiate with foreign leaders?

Military and naval institutions thus exist to make statements about relative power and resolve. In wartime the combatants exchange blows. Think of battles and engagements as statements and replies in an armed conversation. In peacetime the contestants hold fire yet try to project the image of powerful, competent forces that *would* win should some peacetime controversy come to blows. They try to make an imposing impression. If political leaders comport themselves in friendly yet candid fashion while brandishing impressive martial might, they stand a good chance of facing down potential foes while heartening allies and potential allies they would like to recruit to the cause. This is classic Kissingerian statecraft.

Combat capability underwrites everyday diplomacy as surely as it does war on the broad main. This is what President Theodore Roosevelt meant by "speak softly and carry a big stick." He meant for his disciples to conduct themselves with tact and candor while displaying the power to settle matters on their terms should pacific diplomacy go sour. TR touted the world cruise of the U.S. Navy battle fleet (1907–9), or "Great White Fleet," as "the most important service I rendered to peace."[8] The Great White Fleet circumnavigated South America en route to Pacific ports of call such as Sydney and Yokohama. President Roosevelt opined that by showing up in the Far East ready for action, American fighting ships disabused Japanese leaders of any notion that the Imperial Japanese Navy could do to the U.S. Navy what it had done to the Russian Baltic Fleet in 1905: crush a hostile fleet wearied by a prolonged journey into the combat theater without rest, ample supplies, or repairs. He believed parading American power and resolve before Japanese eyes deterred aggression.

Underlying such ventures in armed diplomacy is a truism conveyed by Gen. George S. Patton in his renowned 1944 address to the Third Army: *people love a winner and will not tolerate a loser*. In other words, observers take the measure of two armed forces when they square off, make their best estimate of which would emerge triumphant should combat ensue, and cast their lot with the probable victor. Few will side with losers. It affronts human nature. Worse, entangling oneself with a losing cause means sharing the bitter fruits of defeat. Political and strategic leaders who flourish military implements to good effect—and position themselves in the minds of observers as the likely victors—thus hold the key to success in peacetime strategic competition.

Strategists have long wrestled with the question of how to win without fighting in human competition. The Chinese general Sun Tzu pronounces bloodless victory the "acme of skill."[9] Prussian soldier-scribe Carl von Clausewitz agrees, pointing out that the general need not triumph on the battlefield to win. An army can win by disheartening its opponents or by making them believe they cannot win on likely battlegrounds at a price political leaders or the larger society are willing to pay.[10] Few combatants fight when they despair of their chances of winning. Or they abjure battle when they could win but their goals are not worth the probable cost or hazards to them.

This is what the strategist Edward Luttwak terms "suasion" transcribed to a saltwater setting. Suasion is a term with a Kissingerian flair. It refers to measures taken to persuade others to do things the persuader wants them to do, or to dissuade them from doing things deemed undesirable. During the late Cold War Luttwak penned a short treatise on this subject titled *The Political Uses of Sea Power*. It is necessary reading for any practitioner or student of naval diplomacy. Henry Kissinger plays up the importance of shaping perceptions among antagonists, allies, and third parties. Luttwak explains how to use warships to do it: "'armed suasion' defines all reactions, political or tactical, elicited by all parties—allies, adversaries, or neutrals—to the existence, display, manipulation, or symbolic use of any instrument of military power, whether or not such reactions reflect any deliberate intent of the deploying party. 'Naval suasion' refers to effects evoked by sea-based or sea-related forces."[11] This is a passage packed with content. Luttwak supplements it with specifics. First, naval deployments can be explicitly geared to deter or coerce antagonists or embolden allies or friends. He declares that "any instrument of military power that can be used to inflict damage upon an adversary" or "physically limit his freedom of action" can "affect his conduct, and that of any interested third parties, even if force is never actually used."[12] Navy overseers apply a stimulus, deploying capability in concert with intent in hopes of eliciting a response desired from target audiences.

Second, naval deployments can generate "latent suasion" effects. Warships on scene exert influence regardless of whether commanders or senior officials connect the ships' actions overtly to specific policies, deterrent threats, or promises. Luttwak points out that Cold War commentators typically differentiated between "peacetime presence" missions and battle readiness, as indeed they still do. For him this constitutes a false choice. Presence avails little without visible combat capability. Luttwak maintains that to be effective the ships, warplanes, and armaments deployed must be "seen as potential threats or potential sources of support."[13] These are capability made manifest in Kissinger's terms.

If target audiences interpret naval implements as viable threats or promises, "they influence the behavior of those who deem themselves to be within reach of the forces concerned." It is a fallacy, then, to talk of naval presence as a standalone function. Instead, the presence of combat-ready capabilities on scene casts a "shadow that impinges on the freedom of action of adversaries, because the capabilities perceived can be activated at any time, while the formulation of the intent to use them can be both silent and immediate."[14] Orders from on high could shunt a ship of war from peacetime presence into battle mode in an instant. Observers know that. Ships of war signify intent and resolve. They cast that shadow—and the more striking the peacetime display of force, the longer and darker the shadow.

Luttwak thus finds it "misleading to make any dichotomy between 'peacetime presence' and 'wartime' combat capabilities, since a 'presence' can have no significant effect in the absence of *any* possibility that the transition to war will be made."[15] Audiences have little reason to take threats or promises seriously if they know a navy will not or cannot act on them. In Kissinger's parlance, deterrence, coercion, or reassurance are zero in such situations. Naval diplomats' words carry no weight absent combat capacity.

Third, fleet movements can yield unintended consequences. "Because suasion can only operate through the filters of others' perceptions," says Luttwak, "the exercise of suasion is inherently unpredictable in its results. Routine fleet movements which were not intended to pose a threat may be seen by others as threatening (since the threat is *latent* in the forces themselves). On the other hand, a deliberate but tacit threat may be ignored, or worse, may evoke contrary reactions" (emphasis in original).[16] Strategic competition pits imperfect competitors against one another in a struggle for advantage. In such circumstances the chances of misperceptions, deception, or sheer stubbornness on the part of various audiences are acute. Fleet commanders or officialdom may cast that shadow across others without intending to, they may try to cast it and fail, or they may try to cast one shadow yet cast another.

How to manage perceptions? Through adroit diplomacy from leaders alert to the messages that ship movements can telegraph. Concludes Luttwak, "continuous political guidance of the highest possible quality is a crucial requirement of overseas naval deployments: a modern oceanic fleet needs a political 'radar' as much as it needs the electronic variety." Political advisers should be assigned to naval commands to monitor and adjust "the political 'radiation' emitted by the fleet" while correcting "severe distortions in others' perceptions of the fleet—of its tactical configuration and the underlying political intent of its movements."[17] Advisers help tune in the messages that are broadcast—and improve the likelihood that hearers will interpret them as intended.

Fourth, putting naval deployments in political and strategic context matters. Dispatching a single ship or a compact flotilla has political clout so long as audiences know the combined weight of the navy stands behind it—hence the term "gunboat diplomacy."[18] A small formation acts as a proxy for the navy as a whole. No one expects to overawe anyone with one lightly armed patrol craft, frigate, or littoral combat ship. USS *San Pablo*, the star of Richard McKenna's *The Sand Pebbles*, was an accurate fictional portrayal of real-life gunboats performing diplomatic duty.[19] In fact, the U.S. Navy obtained some of these dilapidated craft from Spain as spoils of the Spanish-American War. They cruised the Yangtze until 1941, impressing few with their combat power.[20] They impressed insofar as Chinese regarded them as talismans of American naval might—in other words, as symbols of the combined power of the U.S. Navy.

A humble show of force might overawe a target audience if the observers are certain an overpowering force will gather on the scene should they prove recalcitrant. It is the job of naval diplomats to impress upon them that this will indeed happen. Small units, then, act as symbols or tokens of political commitment as much as warfighting implements.[21] They sow fear or confidence that the fleet's heavy hitters will arrive on the scene if needed. Power in waiting thus imbues even innocuous craft with menace, helping deter or coerce opponents while cheering allies and friends.

And fifth, target audiences may be inexpert at judging naval combat power, yet their perceptions count all the same. Perverse outcomes can result from peacetime showdowns between fleets. These are battles of perceptions in a real sense. Maintains Luttwak, whichever force most observers believe would have triumphed in wartime triumphs in peacetime—regardless of whether the observers' opinion makes military sense. General Patton's logic of favoring winners while deploring losers comes into play. The objectively weaker competitor can "win" such an encounter if it prevails in the subjective battle of perceptions.

Some of this phenomenon owes to the part high technology now plays in warfare. Weapon systems, observes Luttwak, remain "black boxes" to outside observers until used in high-seas battle, the final arbiter of what does and does not work in naval affairs.[22] Software, big data, and cyberwarfare assume ever greater significance in naval operations—and disguise true capability in the process. Even experts find it difficult to gauge prospective foes' combat potential.

In part, however, misperceptions may stem from the look of a ship, plane, or weapon. Weaponry can appear fearsome while contributing little battle power to a force. Luttwak pointed to the Soviet Navy. The Soviet Union deployed an armada of vessels by the 1970s when he wrote. Many were technologically backward relative to Western navies, but they *looked* mighty impressive. These were big, musclebound ships festooned with sensor arrays and guns. They sported antiship missiles in massive topside launchers, seemingly ready to clobber foes that dared come against them. They exuded "sex appeal."[23]

By the 1980s, by contrast, the U.S. Navy took to deploying missiles in vertical launch cells—in effect, silos embedded in the main deck of a cruiser or destroyer. Vertical launch batteries were nondescript. They looked like panels flush with the deck. American weapons remained out of sight, and thus made little visual impact on the untutored. Vertical launch constituted a major advance in weapons technology. Yet the advantage in perceptions went to the Soviets even though the combat power boasted by their vessels was—in part—illusory.

Mariners and their political masters must attune themselves to these facets of naval diplomacy. There is clearly far more to the diplomatic enterprise than showing up in foreign seaports and going on liberty or meeting with local potentates. This is a political process—and politics is fraught with perceptions and misperceptions, chance and uncertainty, and consequences expected and unexpected. Maritime strategy is the art and science of access. Diplomatic access advances that cause by harnessing naval might to coax foreign partners into granting liberal access and to face down those who might try to circumscribe or forbid it. It behooves seafaring folk to refine their diplomatic prowess alongside seamanship and tactical and technical skills. Kissinger, Luttwak, and even Patton can help them think such matters through.

Police Role

Ken Booth lists the police function second among his naval functions. The slogan emblazoned on the sides of police cruisers everywhere captures the essence of police duty: "to protect and serve." To protect means maintaining public safety and order in the face of lawbreakers. Upholding law and order lets citizens go about their daily business, generating wealth that sustains families and society and provides tax revenue to fund government operations—including a police force. To serve means enhancing public well-being. Police work fosters the health, welfare, and morals of the people. Protecting and serving represent the twin halves of the "police power" embedded in domestic constitutional law.[24]

This arrangement finds a parallel in maritime strategy. No one is sovereign over the entire international system. There is no global authority to wield a monopoly on the use of legitimate force and thus the police power. Thus, individual nations, their navies and coast guards, and affiliated armed forces work together to supply a makeshift substitute. Navies and coast guards underwrite the freedom to use the maritime common for commercial and military purposes, undertaking efforts to enforce what Geoffrey Till calls "good order at sea."[25]

Protecting the distribution link in the maritime supply chain means combating nonstate scourges such as piracy, terrorism, and weapons trafficking. It is part and parcel of enforcing freedom of the sea—the sinew that binds together the liberal system of seagoing trade and commerce on which seafaring states depend for their economic well-being. Small wonder that the 2015 *Asia-Pacific Maritime Security Strategy*, a document published late in the Obama administration, lists freedom of the sea first among the Defense Department's priorities for the nautical domain. It appears starting on page 1 of the strategy. Safeguarding trade goods transiting the sea-lanes constitutes a compelling mutual interest for the oceangoing world. The document adds that U.S. forces need access to coastal regions to respond to crises or disasters.[26] Navies help uphold these vital interests.

Law enforcement at sea is a peculiar type of law enforcement. It requires joint action bringing together navies, coast guards, and other government agencies entrusted with maritime duties, along with combined effort among sea services and agencies from multiple countries. Collaboration among unlike institutions can bring on culture clashes. Ambassador Robert Komer, who headed the civil-military pacification effort in Vietnam, notes that bureaucratic institutions discharge "repertoires" of routine tasks that derive from their main functions. They execute these tasks, machinelike, over and over again in exactly the same way.[27]

Bureaucratic repertoires give rise to disparate organizational worldviews and cultures. At times this makes it difficult for even outwardly similar services such as a navy and a coast guard from the same nation to work together. After all, defeating enemies constitutes the chief purpose of navies while law enforcement and lifesaving constitute coast guards' main reason for being. A chasm in institutional worldviews results. Forging a common outlook on constabulary duty—and thus bolstering harmony of effort—can prove trying even under auspicious circumstances.

The multinational dimension imports politics into law enforcement endeavors. It is not the case that a "global maritime partnership"—U.S. sea-service parlance for combined constabulary operations—automatically comes into being whenever some seaborne menace rears up. Think about impediments to such operations. Except for sea powers that aspire to regional or global reach, coastal states tend to take what happens in their immediate environs more seriously than what transpires in distant waters. They may blanch at making more than a token effort far from home. This is doubly true of developing countries for which economic development is the paramount priority. The upshot: it is hard for political leaders to persuade their constituents to allocate scarce maritime resources to quell lawlessness in someone else's backyard. The problem and the benefits of law enforcement are largely invisible to ordinary folk, while the expense of dispatching ships and other assets is visible and pressing. Constituents may balk at what they regard as waste.

Problems abound even among close allies or partners. Allies routinely fear "abandonment" and "entrapment" by friends.[28] Abandonment refers to the fear of committing to some allied venture, then being left standing alone when an ally downgrades its effort or pulls out of the arrangement because interests or purposes divert its attention elsewhere. Even the U.S.-Japan alliance, among history's closest, suffers from such qualms. Tokyo worries that Washington will exit the security treaty that unites the two countries vis-à-vis a rising China. Japan can compete on more or less equal terms in concert with the United States; it is woefully outmatched in a one-on-one competition—and thus might have to submit to Beijing's demands, just or unjust. For instance, Japanese leaders fretted about the possibility of U.S. abandonment over the Senkaku

Islands for years. It was unclear whether Washington believed the U.S.-Japan Security Treaty applied to uninhabited southwestern islands. At last the Obama administration pledged to help defend the Senkakus—and put Japanese minds at ease.

Entrapment is the opposite fear. One ally worries that too faithful a commitment to another will drag it into adventurism that works against its national interests, purposes, or ideals. It faces a quandary. To cite the U.S.-Japan alliance again, the United States has pledged to defend Taiwan against aggression from the mainland. Japan has no treaty commitment to defend the island, yet its leadership might feel obliged to support U.S. forces for the sake of preserving the alliance with the United States. Tokyo knows it would face a wrathful Beijing after a cross-strait war—regardless of who prevailed. That prospect comprises a deterrent to standing alongside America. Japan might proceed anyway for reciprocity's sake. In other words, Japan would fight to keep the alliance strong and thereby ensure American steadfastness in future contingencies that endangered Japanese interests.

Concerns about abandonment and entrapment thus tinge multinational enterprises of all types. Competitive pressures can also misshape constabulary partnerships or confound them altogether. For instance, it is doubtful proposals to form a U.S.–Japan–China entente to police the Yellow Sea or East China Sea would get far. Would-be partners would harbor misgivings about one another's intentions and deeds.

Or consider the South China Sea, where the U.S. armed forces have long trained, equipped, and held exercises with Southeast Asian armed forces, ostensibly for constabulary missions. Yet China suspects that the United States is using police duty as cover for arming regional forces and uniting a coalition to contain China. Luttwak might add that sea services can pivot from police to combat duty if so ordered. A constabulary arrangement could conceivably balk China's political and strategic aims in a sea that it fancies a Chinese lake. Hence Beijing's wariness.

And then there are functional impediments to acting in unison. Even if the politics works out, partners' navies and coast guards come in all shapes and sizes, are organized differently, and are assigned different mandates by their governments. Disparities in capability further complicate efforts to orchestrate global maritime partnerships. "Interoperability" refers to compatibility between hardware and operating methods within and between armed services. Foreign military sales and multinational exercises help smooth out such troubles, but managing them represents a never-ending challenge for seafarers.

Police work as Washington envisions it confronts even larger obstacles. As Machiavelli claims, founding something new constitutes the most trying act of statesmanship. During the Bush and Obama years the United States embarked on an unprecedented effort to create a multinational steward of maritime security. That is, Washington hoped a standing alliance, coalition, or family of coalitions and partnerships would preside over the common. The two administrations issued maritime strategy documents titled *A Cooperative Strategy for 21st Century Seapower* (2007 and 2015), appealing to coastal states to join forces to quell lawbreaking.

This logic behind this initiative makes perfect sense, but at the same time it demands an effort of world-historical scope. Washington must not underestimate the diplomatic and operational challenges it has taken on. Think about it. For the past half-millennium or thereabouts a single maritime hegemon—Spain, Portugal, Holland, Britain, and now America—has overseen the common. Doing so is straightforward even though it taxes national resources. After all, individual governments and naval services can act with relative ease and clarity of purpose.

U.S. sea-service leaders, however, announced through the *Cooperative Strategy* directives that they intended to found and lead multinational coalitions *and* that they had fewer resources to devote to police endeavors. It is a truism that the ally that chips in the most manpower and hardware gets the dominant say in alliance deliberations. If Washington truly has less to commit to constabulary duty, it cannot expect to set the maritime agenda with the same ease it enjoyed in past coalitions.[29] In short, it is attempting to accomplish something unprecedented and uniquely ambitious from a position of relative weakness.

There is no substitute for making the effort. Upholding secure sea-lanes and preventing resource poaching are pressing tasks on grounds of national self-interest alone. All trading societies benefit from a secure distribution link in the global supply chain, and from reaping the resources allocated to them under the law of the sea. Wooing stakeholders into taking a share of the maritime security burden constitutes a worthy endeavor.

But it is also worthwhile in ways that do not promise such direct payoffs. Naval services render aid and solace following human and natural disasters, for instance. Governments initiate humanitarian missions in part because it is the right thing to do and in part because it wins them legitimacy in the eyes of others. Thus has it always been. Back in 1907 the British diplomat Eyre Crowe wrote an influential missive maintaining, in part, that the Royal Navy furnished the entire seagoing world with maritime security at British expense.[30] Beneficiaries of British-supplied maritime security acquiesced in British maritime supremacy, contended Crowe, because it spared them from raising large fleets of their own to quash brigandage and respond to emergencies. Harvard professor Joseph Nye portrays such exchanges of "international public goods" for legitimacy as part of national "soft power."[31]

Good order at sea is one such public good. Providing it relieves others of the burden for upholding it, earning the provider a measure of forbearance and goodwill. In turn the provider may get its way more easily in international forums in the future, on the logic that goodwill begets more goodwill. Nations do well by doing good, and they advance their own interests in the bargain. This is how soft power works. Constabulary work pays dividends in many ways—but it demands diplomatic and operational dexterity.

Between Police and Military Roles in the Gray Zone

Recent years have underscored that nonstate lawbreakers are not the only enemies of freedom of the sea. In effect some coastal states want to amend the law of the sea to the detriment of nautical freedom. And they intend to do so not through overt territorial conquest but through "gray zone" operations that deliver concrete gains while stopping short of armed conflict. Such operations take place in that shadowland where peace blurs into war. Practitioners of gray-zone strategies use paramilitary forces such as coast guards or maritime militias for geopolitical gain. They sometimes even turn to nonmilitary implements such as fishing trawlers packed with electronic surveillance gear or merchantmen configured to double as minelayers.

It is hard to respond effectively to such tactics. Deploying military force against a coast guard cutter or fishing craft could trigger a diplomatic debacle. The user of force would look like the bully, no matter how just its cause. In fact, gray-zone conflict resembles an incipient insurgency. Notes counterinsurgency specialist David Galula, an incumbent government finds it hard to cope with "cold revolutionary war"—peacetime agitation against an incumbent government—because it remains unclear whether there will be a hot revolutionary war. The political opposition might confine itself to nonviolent protest rather than take up arms. Reluctant to deploy force to crush what might be peaceful political movements, governments commonly succumb to indecision and paralysis.[32] Which precisely the point for practitioners of this murky approach to warfare: it annuls a stronger enemy's material advantages.

In the international realm, likewise, the custodian and protector of an existing order—an order such as the liberal system of maritime trade and commerce that allows the global supply chain to flourish—is conflicted because purveyors of gray-zone strategy deliberately refuse to breach the threshold between uneasy peace and armed conflict. They fire no shots. They may use their hulls to block the path of an opponent's shipping and effectively substitute physical mass for firepower. They refuse to supply a casus belli justifying an armed riposte. They compel the keeper of the status quo to choose between acting first—and bearing the blame for the outbreak of war—and contenting itself with half-measures or inaction. Its leadership must choose between vacillating, thus ceding the initiative, and escalating, thus looking like the aggressor.

In short, gray-zone strategies impose dilemmas on conservators of an existing order. As noted starting in chapter 1, the maritime common is such an order.[33] Much like the New England town common, it belongs to everyone and no one. This is a realm where navies, air forces, and commercial fleets enjoy virtually boundless freedom to use sea and sky. And yet the idea and the reality of the common have come under challenge from coastal states such as China and Russia. Rather than resort to open warfare to abridge freedom of the sea, China has fashioned gray-zone strategies to advance its policies in the China seas. Observes Johns Hopkins professor Hal Brands, this shadowy technique

is best understood as activity that is coercive and aggressive in nature, but that is deliberately designed to remain below the threshold of conventional military conflict and open interstate war. Gray zone approaches are mostly the province of revisionist powers—those actors that seek to modify some aspect of the existing international environment—and the goal is to reap gains, whether territorial or otherwise, that are normally associated with victory in war. Yet gray zone approaches are meant to achieve those gains *without* escalating to overt warfare, *without* crossing established red-lines, and thus *without* exposing the practitioner to the penalties and risks that such escalation might bring. (emphasis in original)[34]

To do so, China employs both naval and nonnaval instruments of maritime power to compel others to do its bidding in the maritime domain. China's way of gray-zone strategy appears founded on creating the semblance of sovereignty over disputed islands, seas, and skies. To go back to Max Weber's definition once again, sovereignty involves imposing a monopoly on the use of legitimate force within certain lines on the map called borders. Beijing imposes a preponderance of armed forces of all types and dares others to reverse it. It has constructed naval and military forces able to overpower any local competitor and has built and armed islands to lend their own backing to the mix. Chinese leaders hope legitimacy will follow their effort to master regional waters as competitors resign themselves to the new normal.

This audacious strategy stages an assault not just on China's Asian neighbors but on the law of the sea and thus on the liberal maritime order as a whole. And yet Beijing makes unassuming forces—the China Coast Guard, fishing craft, merchantmen—the face of its strategy. Only if Asian capitals buck Beijing's pretensions to sovereignty will it deploy conventional military firepower. As Edward Luttwak might remind us, physically weak craft represent symbols of overwhelming might lying in wait over the horizon. They may not be students of Luttwak, but South China Sea claimants are perfectly aware of this. Thus, Beijing boasts considerable capacity to deter or coerce Asian capitals—even if warships never appear at scenes of impact.

Even if sitting over the horizon, then, China's navy casts a long shadow through latent suasion. Commentators on Chinese maritime strategy dwell principally on traditional implements of sea power—namely, the People's Liberation Army Navy and the shore-based arsenal whose firepower backs it up. This is natural. Arguably, though, the chief peacetime function of high-end weaponry is to furnish a backstop for unglamorous vessels prowling the gray zone. Nor is this relationship anything new despite the fancy new catchphrase. China's leadership has long regarded fishing fleets, commercial shipping, and law enforcement services as a paramilitary arm of sea power. If it can mold events at sea, then, it is an instrument of sea power for China.

Beijing thus takes a genuinely maritime approach to strategic competition. How to police an expanse claimed by a domineering coastal state remains to be determined, if indeed it is possible. As chapter 1 shows, four centuries ago the English jurist John Selden proclaimed that strong coastal states could own the sea, governing water space as though it were land. If, like Selden, China or like-minded coastal states sincerely view offshore waters as territory where domestic law prevails—not the law of the sea—then in their eyes collaborating on maritime security would be like inviting foreign armies or militias onto their soil to help police it. No power that sees itself as strong and virile could countenance such a thing.

Retired Australian commodore Sam Bateman observes that a host of "wicked problems" bedevil the Asia–Pacific region. He defines them as "pressing and highly complex issues for policy formulation that involve many causal factors and high levels of disagreement about the nature of a problem and the best way to handle it."[35] Such problems confound ready solutions, says Bateman, not merely because they intersect with many issues but because they engage "fundamental differences" between contenders with "deeply held convictions about the correctness of their own position." Agreement "invariably" demands that disputants "change their mindsets and behavior." He describes the Asia–Pacific as "awash with wicked problems" such as "conflicting maritime claims and managing the risks of greater naval activity in the region."[36]

Southeast Asia is a microcosm of the Asia-Pacific. In Geoffrey Till's parlance, cross-cutting interests between the dominion, good order at sea, and transportation domains magnify the difficulty of resolving disputes—and render amity and cooperation fleeting. Embroiling wicked problems with gray-zone strategies with routine security functions makes the enclosed, crowded, resource-rich waters of the South China Sea a crucible of disputes and controversies. Multinational policing of regional waters and shores verges on impossible under the present circumstances.

Nor is the situation likely to improve as Chinese military power swells and as Beijing's capacity to act as a spoiler—and enforce its own style of good order at sea through unilateral action—swells with it. Worse still, Beijing's gray-zone strategy could inspire imitators if it succeeds. Russia has conceived its own variant of gray-zone strategy, laying claim to the Sea of Azov, an enclave in the Black Sea east of the Crimean Peninsula, and to the Northern Sea Route that skirts the Russian Arctic coast.[37] Iran has long asserted special prerogatives in the Strait of Hormuz, a critical artery that connects the Persian Gulf with the Indian Ocean and runs along Iranian shores.[38] If Beijing manages to make itself sovereign in the China seas, there is no reason in principle that Moscow and Tehran cannot do the same in their own nearby seas. How to execute constabulary work when a powerful state is the antagonist thus poses a strategic challenge of the first order. This challenge is here to stay.

Military Role

If peacetime strategic competition seeks negative aims—to keep an adversary from seizing something it wants—wartime strategy can be geared to either negative or positive aims. A combatant pursuing positive aims wants to wrest something from its opponent, while the opponent wants to keep that from happening—and thus crafts negative aims.[39] Carl von Clausewitz points out that diplomatic intercourse need not come to a halt once the contestants take up arms and start trading blows. Nevertheless, adding exchanges of fire to the policy mix transforms strategic competition. The virtual war of nerves and perceptions profiled in Kissinger's and Luttwak's writings gives way to impassioned interactions whereby actual battles and engagements substitute for diplomatic notes. Rather than make hypothetical claims about relative strength and weakness, they submit to the verdict of arms on the battlefield—much as scientists put their theories to the test during field trials. Reality becomes the arbiter of ideas about hardware, tactics, and operations. In a sense, exclaims Clausewitz, war is "just another expression" of the combatants' thoughts, or "another form of speech or writing."[40] It is diplomatic interchange with the addition of warlike means and methods.

Notice, then, that Booth's military function forms the foundation for everything naval services do in the realms of naval diplomacy and police duty. Peacetime diplomatic clout stems from perceptions that a navy will be the probable victor in a hypothetical sea fight. Perceptions of prowess and determination lend power to diplomats' words. Similarly, military efficacy is a necessary ingredient for frustrating the designs of state enemies of freedom of the sea. And even in the strictly constabulary domain, coast guards must be equipped to overpower nonstate aggressors such as brigands, terrorists, and gunrunners. Force effectively employed is the common denominator among these enterprises.

We at last turn to how navies help their fellow armed forces and their larger societies prevail in struggles for dominion. No longer does a force settle for casting a shadow across diplomatic relations. Commanders strive to impose their political masters' will by force of arms. We thus dip down toward the operational and tactical levels of war while keeping our gaze fixed firmly on grand strategic success.

Here a nod to British soldier and theorist B. H. Liddell Hart is in order. A veteran of trench warfare in World War I, Liddell Hart longed to avoid future bloodlettings of the type witnessed on the Western Front from 1914 to 1918. He was the forefather of the contemporary concept of grand strategy. As noted at the outset of chapter 1, this refers to the art and science of fashioning diplomatic, informational, military, and economic power into a sharp strategic implement for political gain.

Alfred Thayer Mahan's concept of maritime strategy as an enterprise aimed at commercial, political, and military access to the rimlands falls squarely into this genre. Maritime strategy is a variety of grand strategy—and the variety of choice for coastal societies with the right stuff to succeed on the bounding main. As such, and even though his writings antedated Liddell Hart's by years, Mahan shares the British thinker's view that strategic excellence lies in engineering "a better state of peace—even if only from your own point of view."[41]

The two writers beseech statesmen to improve the state of peace through nonviolent means if they can, and to fight only if they must. For Liddell Hart, strategy is as much an attitude as it is a method of wielding national power for strategic and political ends. It is the habit of taking the long view rather than dwelling on the minutiae of martial affairs. Like Sun Tzu, for whom he professes limitless admiration, Liddell Hart strongly prefers to win without fighting, sparing his country the costs and ravages of war. If bloodless victory proves impossible, he exhorts political and strategic leaders to "take account of and apply the power of financial pressure, of diplomatic pressure, of commercial pressure, and, not least of ethical pressure, to weaken the opponent's will." Such a broad perspective boosts the likelihood of strategic success. And "while the horizon of strategy is bounded by the war, grand strategy looks beyond the war to the subsequent peace."[42]

So war is about peace for Liddell Hart. In the realm of maritime strategy, a better state of peace would restore commercial, political, and military access while creating ambient conditions favoring access into the future. Access thus should be maritime strategists' north star. Peering back into the age of Mahan, the tenets of U.S. maritime strategy have long involved obtaining and defending access while managing the Eurasian rimlands to keep any overbearing power or alliance from dominating them—and thus amassing the naval and military resources to constitute a threat to the Western Hemisphere.[43] Furthermore, the United States took over as superintendent of the system of oceangoing trade and commerce after 1945. Erstwhile maritime hegemon Great Britain had exhausted itself beating back the Central Powers in World War I and the Axis in World War II. Britain's recessional left America as the only candidate standing.[44]

American primacy at sea also connoted commanding the marginal seas ringing Eurasia. As chapter 2 notes, during World War II the geopolitics specialist Nicholas Spykman contemplated how sea powers can mold events along foreign coasts and inland. Surveying British imperial history, Spykman concluded that the British Empire was successful because the Royal Navy ruled the "girdle of marginal seas," semi-enclosed waters swaddling the Eurasian supercontinent. Maritime supremacy allowed Britain to project power into the heartland from these offshore havens. For him the sea represents a staging area for exerting influence on dry land.

Expanses such as the Baltic Sea, Bay of Bengal, and South China Sea take on outsized importance in Spykman's scheme. If controlling peripheral seas empowered the Royal Navy to administer a globe-spanning empire, it is also how the U.S. Navy and affiliated joint forces have administered an informal empire since World War II. Navies accomplish little in the rimlands without access to marginal waters.[45] They cannot radiate power ashore unless they can close within reach of shipboard weaponry to bombard landward targets or execute amphibious landings.

At the Naval War College, we often ask our students whether they prefer Mahan or Julian Corbett as a maritime strategic theorist. In so doing we deliberately pose a false choice. The two scribes had different agendas and wrote for different audiences. They naturally pitched their messages differently. As an Englishman, Corbett saw little need to explain why his government should construct a great battle fleet. It already possessed the world's finest. As an American, Mahan wrote in large measure to convince his countrymen they needed their first serious fleet. Accordingly, Mahan expounds on the purposes for sea power whereas Corbett investigates the mechanics for putting a battle fleet that already rides the waves to work for wartime strategic gain. His writings add texture and subtlety to sea-power theory, whereas Mahan billed the U.S. Navy as a bludgeon for walloping hostile fleets in head-on battle.

Adm. J. C. Wylie, another veteran of the Naval War College faculty, interpreted the two historians' works in similar fashion, opining that Mahan excelled at explaining the *policy* impelling sea power while Corbett set forth a theater *strategy* aimed at winning sea fights and exploiting the results to advance larger purposes. Says Wylie: "Mahan sensed it before Corbett and wrote all around and about it, but never did quite put his finger on it. He did not summarize his thoughts in clear, inclusive general terms, nor did he succinctly set forth a model strategy for maritime warfare. What Mahan became famous for, and quite properly so, was his recognition of the role of sea power as a basis for national policy."[46]

Mahan tried to do it all, exploring the purposes impelling the quest for sea power *and* methods for waging war at sea. Or, as historians Harold Sprout and Margaret Sprout put it, Mahan devised a "philosophy of sea power . . . a theory of national prosperity and destiny founded upon a program of mercantilistic imperialism" as well as a "theory of naval strategy and defense." Corbett settled for crafting—to borrow the Sprouts' words—a "theory of naval strategy and defense" to guide an established hegemon such as Great Britain.[47]

Closely related to this difference in outlooks is the question of whether victory at sea is a goal in its own right or simply a precursor to what comes after. Mahan devotes his energy mainly to explaining why wresting away command of vital expanses is crucial. Smash the enemy fleet, he suggests, and laudable results will follow. He downplays the specifics of how to reap strategic dividends from operational victory. For example, he quotes George Monk, the first Duke of Albemarle: "When Monk said *the nation that would rule upon the sea must always attack*, he set the key-note to England's naval policy. Had French rulers 'consistently breathed the same spirit' during the War of American Independence, when France allied itself with the American colonists, the venture 'might have ended sooner and better than it did'—both for France and the colonists" (my emphasis).[48] Conservative French statecraft came off a poor second best to British entrepreneurship.

For his part, Corbett maintains that the aim of naval operations is to shape events on land as part of a maritime strategy prosecuted in concert with ground forces (and today, he would doubtless add, air forces as well). In wartime, he maintains, the paramount concern of maritime strategy is to "determine the mutual relations of your army and navy in a plan of war."[49] Corbett was a prophet of "jointness" or "jointery"—meaning deploying one military service in concert with others as part of a cohesive effort—long before these neologisms were invented.[50] Molding events on shore is paramount for him: "Since men live upon the land and not upon the sea, great issues between nations at war have always been decided—except in the rarest cases—either by what your army can do against your enemy's territory and national life or else by the fear of what the fleet makes it possible for your army to do."[51] In other words, naval war is merely an enabler for strategic success—not an end in itself, as it appears to be for Mahan. For Corbett as for Spykman and Wylie, the sea constitutes a medium whereby strategists and tacticians project influence ashore. Wylie agrees that it was Corbett who "first described in a clear and structurally complete form" that it was important to control the sea in order to control events on shore. People live on dry earth; hence, quarrels among nations are settled there.

Maritime strategists must ponder such philosophical questions. They should also entertain the possibility that they can mix and match concepts from the strategic canon to reach a kind of synthesis. Offensively minded readers might prefer Mahan's teachings across the board. He always espouses risking the fleet—provided naval officialdom has done its job and outfitted the fleet to fight with decent chances of success. But it is possible to read Mahan for insight into larger purposes yet incline to Corbett as the more sophisticated analyst of how to use naval power to win wars. This is how I see things. Mahan is the theorist of the stronger navy and lusts to do battle at the earliest instant, while Corbett devotes much of his work *Some Principles of Maritime Strategy* to explaining how the weaker navy can win given time, ingenuity, and operational dexterity. This is a more supple vision, and it comports better with reality.

The question that obsessed naval specialists during the age of Mahan and Corbett was this: should fleet commanders seek a decisive battle at the outset of war? How the maritime scholars answer it throws the difference between their perspectives into stark relief. Mahan says *yes*. Commanders should carry the fight to the enemy in enemy home waters at the earliest opportunity. As chapters 1 and 2 show, the peacetime Mahanian script for amassing sea power involves building a fleet able to compete on even terms or better with the largest hostile force it is likely to encounter. In wartime Mahan countenances risking that fleet under almost all circumstances. He is venturesome in the extreme.

Mahan believed fervently that commanders must dare much when bidding for maritime mastery. They should concentrate the "overbearing power" manifest in the fleet at the outset of war and seek battle as soon as possible. Mahan takes French admirals to task for apathy and strategic drift during the American War of Independence, when the French navy bore most of the brunt of the allied war effort at sea. In particular, he faults French seamen for focusing on seizing British-held islands in the Caribbean Sea. They misdirected their efforts at the same time a strong Royal Navy fleet remained at large in regional seaways and able to contest French command.[52] French commanders had their priorities reversed.

Vanquish the enemy fleet and you vanquish the enemy's territorial holdings, Mahan seems to say: "if naval superiority is to be maintained, the enemy's navy must be crushed."[53] British islands would have withered on the vine once the British fleet lay in ruins. French victory at sea would have denied island garrisons seaborne supplies and reinforcements, and they would have fallen into French hands one by one. The lesson from Mahan is that good things follow when naval commanders make defeating the foe's fleet the focal point of their endeavors. They must never get their priorities askew.

Should a hostile fleet refuse to fight a decisive battle, writes Mahan, the fleet should box it in by imposing a naval blockade. Though less satisfactory than sinking the foe's fleet, confining it to port takes it off the field of battle so long as the quarantine remains tight. This expedient was sometimes necessary. He notes, for example, that the French navy generally refused to come out to duel Royal Navy blockading forces or the main British fleet during the French Revolutionary and Napoleonic

Wars, the prolonged contest that furnished Mahan and Corbett much of their historical grounding. Conserving the fleet instead of risking it obsessed French naval magnates.

A blockade tamps down the threat to the sea-lanes for a time, and Mahan pronounces that a good thing. But it ranks a distant second on his list of strategic preferences, behind seeking battle. And for ample reason. Blockades tax naval power and impose severe opportunity costs. Rendering a blockade effective demands a substantial share of the navy if not the whole force. It also commonly induces the blockading fleet to disperse. Fleet overseers must station a squadron off each enemy seaport or perhaps mount a "distant blockade" along a distended defense perimeter that encloses the entire coastline.[54] Such measures thin out battle strength if an engagement does take place.

Blockades can work. For instance, the Royal Navy suffocated the American economy by the closing stages of the War of 1812. This debacle inspired Mahan to advocate the construction of a battle fleet to prevent such a thing from happening again. Lord Horatio Nelson and his comrades kept the French navy at bay for decades of war against Revolutionary and Napoleonic France.[55] And the Royal Navy imprisoned the German High Seas Fleet in the North Sea with a distant blockade during World War I. Shutting the English Channel and the gap separating Scotland from Norway sufficed for British purposes. The cordon worked because the British Isles formed a solid, impassable segment of the line.

The British fleet merely had to seal off the segments to either end—a manageable job. As a result, the Royal Navy saw little need to station ships off German harbors where they might run afoul of sea mines, submarines, or surface torpedo craft. Seldom is geography that kind to a blockading fleet. The problem with dividing the fleet into smaller and smaller niblets of combat power is that it subjects each detachment to defeat by a locally stronger enemy force. Trying to be strong everywhere places a force at risk of being strong nowhere. A weaker enemy could mass most or all of its forces someplace along the perimeter and puncture it. The demand to attenuate combat power to hold a protracted line constitutes the timeless—and inescapable—dilemma of perimeter defense.

So commanders should relish neither option. Lord Nelson contended that blockade duty did the Royal Navy good: British mariners were constantly at sea perfecting their craft while the French foe languished in port, losing its edge. Still, both close and distant blockades pin down, scatter, and tire the fleet patrolling offshore, and thus entail burdensome opportunity costs. Ships enforcing a blockade are not doing more worthwhile things they might be doing to advance the cause elsewhere, such as escorting convoys, seeking out and destroying enemy detachments that may have slipped through the cordon, and on and on. There is a heavy penalty to pay when an antagonist refuses to fight.

And this seems to complete the Mahanian script for winning maritime wars. Mahan is the theorist of the stronger contender. Enterprising naval commanders mass the fleet at the outset of war, make the enemy's coast their operational frontier, and seek a decisive fleet action. Failing that, they imprison the enemy's fleet in port and postpone a reckoning. This is sound guidance so far as it goes, but it leaves much unsaid. Julian Corbett has much to contribute to any conversation about the whys and wherefores of sea combat. His script is more freeform, and it instructs the lesser as well as the stronger pugilist.

It is worth pointing out that many naval officers and enthusiasts of Corbett's day branded him a heretic. Royal Navy officers greeted Mahan's advocacy of offense, which reaffirmed their longstanding preference. They scorned Corbett for contemplating operations that did *not* search out decisive battle right away. An approach that allowed for defensive as well as offensive operations ran counter to the ethos permeating the

Royal Navy old guard. They found it unsatisfying. Nor did Corbett do much to conciliate them. He went out of his way to lampoon contemporary dogma. Of the maxim "the enemy's coast is our frontier," he told one audience at Portsmouth: "You might as well try to plan a campaign by singing 'Rule, Britannia.'"[56]

Corbett pronounces truisms a poor substitute for imaginative strategic thought. Such maxims appeal to the strong, yet Corbett pointed out—correctly—that not even the Royal Navy at the zenith of its power could make itself superior to all enemies at every place on the map at every time. And the navy did not always stand at the apex of its power. Fallacious policy could be at fault. Parliament may have let the overall size of the navy run down, as it did after Britain's smashing yet ruinously expensive victory over France in the Seven Years' War (1756–63).[57] By the American War of Independence, the Royal Navy was no longer equal to the combined fleets of France and Spain as per British tradition. Neglect cost the British dearly. "After France in 1778 and Spain in 1779 joined the war against Great Britain," writes historian Russell Weigley, "the British had to treat the American mainland as a secondary theater. Since their global triumph in the Seven Years War, they had complacently allowed their naval strength to wither so badly that the Admiralty could no longer guarantee the home islands against invasion when threatened by the combined fleets of the Bourbon monarchies."[58] America was relegated to a secondary theater in the American war owing to feckless naval policy. Or operational imperatives could place the navy at a momentary disadvantage. The navy could remain superior in numbers on the whole, yet senior commanders might find it necessary to detach squadrons on errands to different places. Dispersing strength could leave an individual force at a local disadvantage vis-à-vis a lesser but concentrated adversary such as the French navy. It could also leave the main fleet at a disadvantage until outlying detachments returned to add their mass and firepower to the effort.

In short, Corbett envisaged countless reasons the Royal Navy might find itself temporarily outmatched at some critical place and time. Rather than deny reality, he thought ahead about how a locally inferior force could play for time. Time was what commanders might need to mass forces, generate new strength, or weaken the adversary. If their efforts succeeded, they would reverse the balance of forces. The Royal Navy would win a Mahanian triumph, albeit belatedly rather than instantly.

And this makes perfect sense. To prevail, the weak have to fight smarter, more cunningly, and more patiently than the strong, who can afford to throw resources at problems. While Corbett voiced fealty to the Mahanian idea that navies should seek the decisive engagement early on—"nine times out of ten the maxim of seeking out the enemy's fleet, &c., is sound and applicable," he confessed—he spent much time and ink pondering what to do on that one occasion out of ten when the maxim proved unsound and inapplicable.[59]

First, he contested the Mahanian concept of maritime command, which connotes absolute control for all time. The sheer size of the sea rules out such control. Command of the sea exists by degrees. Seldom is it absolute or permanent in the Mahanian sense, even though permanent control ought to remain the commanders' goal. More apostasy from Corbett: he opined that canvassing maritime history shows that "the most common situation in naval war is that neither side has the command; that the normal position is not a commanded sea, but an uncommanded sea. The mere assertion . . . that the object of naval warfare is to get command of the sea actually connotes the proposition that the command is normally in dispute."[60] Mahan thus outlines an ideal case that navies seek but seldom attain. Corbett explains how to conduct operations when the ideal case eludes naval commanders.

Second, Corbett widened his gaze to encompass all important sea-lanes, not just waters contested by an enemy battle fleet. For him the point of naval strategy is to control "communications," meaning the ability to transit the sea-lanes unharmed by enemy forces. Though often necessary and always desirable, demolishing the enemy battle fleet constitutes a subsidiary concern for strategists. "Command of the sea," according to Corbett, "means nothing but the control of maritime communications, whether for commercial or military purposes. The object of naval warfare is control of communications."[61] Control of physical space—water space—represents his uppermost concern. Enemy forces are secondary for him.

This claim conforms to Corbett's taxonomy of fleet design (covered in chapter 2). He proclaims that cruisers—not capital ships—are the chief executors of naval operations. They are cheap, adequately armed, and affordable in bulk, extending the navy's reach to police communications. Sentinel ships can be scattered along the sea-lanes to good effect. They control water space. Only when the enemy battle fleet threatens friendly control of communications does the decisive fleet action become the overriding aim of naval warfare. "The true function of the battle-fleet," proclaims Corbett, "is to protect cruisers and flotilla at their special work" of protecting friendly shipping and interdicting enemy shipping along sea routes important to commerce and the war effort.[62]

The "true maxim" of sea combat, then, is not *the enemy's coast is our frontier* but this: "The primary object of the fleet is to secure communications, and if the enemy's fleet is in a position to render them unsafe it must be put out of action."[63] Properly deployed, the battle fleet waits in reserve or mounts a blockade if the enemy battle fleet refuses to fight or refrains from attacking friendly communications. For the time being, communications are safe for maritime traffic—which is the point of wartime strategy.

Third, Corbett breaks down nautical command into stages and insists that a navy can achieve its operational goals short of absolute command—sometimes far short. Commanders waste time, effort, and resources when they bid for absolute command but can get by without it. Corbett defines sea control in terms of time and geographic space. The passage where he lays out his brief is worth quoting at length: "Command may exist in various states or degrees, each of which has its special possibilities and limitations. *It may be general or local, and it may be permanent or temporary.* General command may be permanent or temporary, but mere local command, except in very favorable geographical conditions, should scarcely ever be regarded as more than temporary, since normally it is always liable to interruption from other theaters so long as the enemy possesses an effective naval force" (my emphasis).[64]

While incapacitating or destroying the enemy battle fleet remains desirable, then, a navy can often make do with lesser degrees of control. Even permanent general control does not mean the enemy can do nothing—it simply means the enemy can do nothing effective to confound friendly use of the sea.[65] If, say, the goal of an operation is to land troops on contested shores, and if the amphibious force and its escorts can clear a corridor to the landing beaches for long enough to deposit the troops and their supplies ashore, then that might be enough control for the force to accomplish its goals on land—in other words, its crucial goals—despite the fact that the adversary's fleet remains undefeated.

As historian Samuel Eliot Morison points out, this was precisely the case during the Solomon Islands campaign of 1942–43. The Imperial Japanese Navy held an advantage in night combat during the early stages of the Solomon campaign while the U.S. Navy ruled the day. Owing to asymmetry, reports Morison, "a curious tactical situation oped" around the contested island of Guadalcan virtual exchange of sea mastery every twelve hours." The U.S. Navy "ruled the waves from sunup to sundown" and took the opportunity to run in supplies to U.S. Marines defending the airfield on Guadalcanal. "But as the tropical twilight performed a quick fadeout . . . big ships cleared out like frightened children. . . . Then the Japanese took over" and ran in their own reinforcements and supplies.[66] Alternating sea control fueled six months of tough fighting.

Guadalcanal thus attests to the potential and shortcomings of partial temporary command of the sea. A navy can fulfill its ends on land if unable to win permanent or general command. For a while two contending navies did it in the Solomons. But Corbett takes his case even further, declaring that a force could make do without *any* degree of command. He admits that logic indicates that a navy must win command before exercising it. Things must happen in their proper sequence. How could it be otherwise? At the same time, though, he insists that war is "not conducted by logic, and the order of proceeding which logic prescribes cannot always be adhered to in practice . . . owing to the special conditions of naval warfare, extraneous necessities intrude themselves which make it inevitable that operations for exercising command should accompany as well as follow operations for securing command."[67]

In this not strictly logical affair, in other words, a navy might have to exercise command before winning it—presumably in a small patch of sea for a short time. Imperatives on land might demand such high-risk gambits. Corbett offers few hints at ders should pull off such a feat. Presum- them to predicate their actions on stealth, maneuver, evading rather than confront- l foe. War is a topsy-turvy undertaking s combatants to hazard counterintuitive lismays mariners—but it does them no good to ignore discomfiting realities about their profession. In this sense Corbett is as much of a risk-taker as Mahan.

These deliberations prompted Corbett to propose a tripartite scheme for winning control of the sea. As he sees it, the fight for command does not unfold in phases, precisely. He outlines options for both the stronger contender and the contender that finds itself temporarily outgunned and has to overcome its inferiority to prevail. He first genuflects to Mahanian strategies. Commanders of the more powerful fleet should indeed seek out a decisive fleet engagement at the onset of war or levy a blockade to nullify the enemy fleet. Swift offensive action remains the most direct, most convenient, and most final way to win a war. Destroy an industrial-age fleet and it will not soon be rebuilt.

Offense represents the natural preference for a dominant navy—a navy like the Royal Navy during the age of Corbett and Mahan or the U.S. Navy today. If superior naval might already exists, it only makes sense to concentrate it for action and deploy it to defeat inferior foes. Disposing of enemy resistance entitles the victor to operate free-range naval and merchant fleets throughout the war zone and beyond. It is "only natural" for maritime hegemons to think this way, says Corbett. So long as lawmakers find it prudent to field a preeminent fleet, chances are mariners' preference for offense "will also be maintained."[68]

In the course of this discussion Corbett grapples with a special problem that sometimes vexes the strong: how to compel a weaker antagonist to risk its battle fleet when it prefers to preserve that fleet. His remedy: attack something the foe prizes so much that it must defend it despite conservative leanings. Corbett presents the example of the three seventeenth-century Anglo-Dutch naval wars. The Dutch navy started off these intermittent conflicts as the stronger force, but its commanders stopped offering battle as the century wore on and Dutch supremacy waned. The Royal Navy's solution? To raid mercantile shipping on which the Netherlands depended for commerce and communications with the overseas Dutch Empire. The Royal Navy deliberately presented its nemesis the awful choice between fighting at a disadvantage and surrendering the empire.[69] The Dutch fought despite forbidding odds—and ultimately lost despite some rousing feats of arms.

Corbett's most intriguing discourse comes when he puts himself in the shoes of the weak and mulls how to dispute a stronger enemy's maritime command. Commanders of a "fleet in being," he maintains, still have options while their navy remains weaker on the whole or fragmented among various points on the map. He groups those options under the umbrella of "active defense."[70] The essence of the concept is that weaker contenders need not and should not shelter passively out of harm's way in hopes that the mere existence of a fleet-in-being will cow the enemy. Instead the weak should take matters into their own hands—searching out opportunities to land offensive tactical blows and, over time, make themselves stronger relative to the foe.

A lesser contender can harass the foe through asymmetric tactics such as torpedo or mine attacks (or missile launches, in the contemporary environment), cutting into its superiority bit by bit. Or, as noted time and again, the weak can assemble to make themselves stronger than the fraction of the enemy force they expect to encounter at a particular place and time. Concentrating helps them mount what Corbett calls "minor offensive operations."[71] Enterprising commanders can win offensive tactical engagements even while the enemy remains stronger on the whole—and in the process can whittle down the enemy's margin of strategic superiority.

Indeed, proclaims Corbett, "True Defensive means waiting for a chance to strike." Offense is the soul of defense. The "strength and the essence of the defensive is the counter-stroke," while defensive measures "will always threaten or conceal an attack."[72] He exhorts commanders who find themselves temporarily outnumbered or outgunned:

> If you are not relatively strong enough to assume the offensive, assume the defensive till you become so—
> (1) Either by inducing the enemy to weaken himself by attacks or otherwise;
> (2) Or by increasing your own strength, by developing new forces or securing allies.[73]

Defense is an expedient. Once strong enough, the fleet goes on the offensive and follows the Mahanian script.

It is worth accenting the multinational dimension of active defense. Lesser antagonists have supplemented their naval power though alliances and partnerships throughout history. They do so in a variety of ways. Allies made common cause at sea during the world wars, aggregating their naval power in a partnership of equals. In effect, classical Sparta, an infantry powerhouse, borrowed a fleet from Persia to overcome the vaunted Athenian navy. British leaders feared Nazi Germany would steal a fleet from France after the downfall of France in 1940. And on the reciprocal side, breaking a foe's maritime alliances or preventing them from coming into being weakens the foe to one's own benefit.

Active defense, then, is a technique for balking a stronger enemy's strategy and chipping away at that enemy's strength while bolstering one's own strength as a precursor to a final reckoning. Corbett proffers the example of Arthur Herbert, the Earl of Torrington and commander of the Royal Navy's Home Fleet in 1690, when an Anglo-Dutch alliance squared off against France. The French navy sought to land troops in Ireland to make trouble for Britain there. Although the Home

Fleet was weaker than the French fleet, Torrington found he could frustrate French designs by clinging to the French force. In other words, he shadowed the foe while refusing to close to gunnery range for battle.[74]

Torrington's fleet was too weak to defeat the French outright, yet it was strong enough that the French commander, Anne-Hilarion de Costentin, the Comte de Tourville, could not risk ordering his transports inshore to execute an amphibious landing. So Tourville forewent the landings—and Torrington achieved his goals without hazarding a fleet engagement. Corbett salutes him for "a plan conceived on the best principles of defense—waiting till the acquisition of fresh force justified a return to the offensive."[75] He also castigates the English Crown for subsequently ordering Torrington to initiate a fleet battle against the superior foe. The leadership mistook sage if inglorious strategy off Ireland for timidity, took tactical matters into its own hands, and saw the Home Fleet mauled at the Battle of Beachy Head, an encounter it stood little chance of winning.[76]

The Beachy Head debacle was at once needless and foreseeable. A successful active defense sees the weak augment their combat power while degrading the antagonist's power. The trendlines carry the competitors toward a crossover point beyond which the erstwhile weak outmatch the erstwhile strong—and can best them in a fleet action that would make Mahan's heart glow. *This*—not a thoughtless quest for early battle—is how a fleet-in-being prevails. U.S. strategists should ponder how to enlist Corbett's insights should they find themselves temporarily outgunned in the future. They should also ponder how weaker antagonists might harness Corbettian insights when they confront the U.S. Navy.[77]

It is worth affixing a postscript to Corbett's musings on how to seize the trident. It is easy to assume, with Mahan, that battle is purely a matter for capital ships, and that knocking out heavy combatants decides the outcome. Strategists wring their hands over the possibility of attacks on American aircraft carriers, for instance. This is a matter of grave concern for sure. But savvy foes could attack other, softer components comprising the infrastructure of U.S. naval power. For instance, disabling combat logistics ships ferrying fuel, ammunition, or stores to the American fleet would cripple it within days. Even a nuclear-powered carrier would find itself impotent once deprived of jet fuel to power its fighters and support aircraft. Attacks on logistics could produce a "mission kill" against a carrier group, depriving the force of its capacity to execute its combat missions.

Or one opponent could attack another's naval bases if they lie within missile or aircraft range. In 1941 the Imperial Japanese Navy's carrier strike force had to steam across thousands of miles of stormy ocean to get at the U.S. fleet base in Hawaii. Today's counterparts to Pearl Harbor lie within easy weapons range of potential foes. A regional antagonist such as China could hammer crucial facilities in Japan or Guam without dispatching a ship or warbird. The People's Liberation Army fields a force of truck-launched ballistic missiles able to reach American bases from Chinese soil.[78] In fact, skirting American strengths is an obvious choice for such antagonists. One imagines Corbett would nod in agreement given his concern about the superempowered flotilla. Antiship missiles carry the technological asymmetries that bewildered him to their utmost.

Going after logistics rather than capital ships is hardly a novel idea. Historian Craig Symonds notes approvingly that Royal Navy warplanes took the time to demolish Italian logistics nodes during their November 1940 air raid on the seaport of Taranto, Italy.[79] They exploited the Italian navy's logistical deficits, especially woefully deficient fuel supplies. Japanese pilots missed a similar opportunity at Pearl Harbor a year later. They concentrated their fire on the U.S. fleet, leaving the infrastructure needed to rebuild and support that fleet mostly unscathed. They could have taken out the drydocks that would refit most of the damaged vessels. They could have taken out the fleet's fuel supply. But they didn't. When Adm. Chester Nimitz arrived to assume command of the Pacific Fleet in December 1941, he marveled at the opportunity Japanese aviators had missed. He promptly started putting that infrastructure to use fighting back. There is more way than one to dismantle an opponent's Mahanian sea-power chain, and Japan missed its chance to do so vis-à-vis the United States in the Pacific.

Exploiting hard-won command constitutes the final phase in Corbett's scheme. Recognizing that no victory is likely to extinguish enemy power entirely, he urges commanders to disperse assets throughout the sea-lanes as broadly as possible so long as they remain close enough to concentrate their strength against residual enemy forces that may try to harry shipping. Managing concentration and dispersal represents "the greater part of practical strategy" for Corbett, as indeed it is for Mahan and other masters of strategy: "The object of a naval concentration . . . will be to cover the widest possible area, and to preserve at the same time elastic cohesion, so as to secure rapid condensations of any two or more of the parts of the organism, and in any part of the area to be covered, at the will of the controlling mind; and above all, a sure and rapid condensation of the whole at the strategical center."[80]

To be sure, this guidance applies across all phases of a conflict. Fleets that have blockaded their foes in port spread out as necessary to bar the gate separating hostile shipping from the high seas. Fleets whose opponents refuse to fight a decisive battle also spread out to police the sea, subject to massing quickly—springing back into shape as though attached by a rubber band—when the time for battle comes. But the problem is particularly acute when cruisers scatter across the sea-lanes, where they could be overpowered even by fugitive vessels or detachments from the enemy fleet. Determining how to deploy heavy forces to succor cruisers or the flotilla is critical to making full use of maritime command—just as it is to winning it.

Special Case: "Cumulative" Operations

A fundamental question on which the masters differ is whether sea power wins wars in itself. Mahan thinks so; he deems it a decisive force in history dating back to classical antiquity.[81] Corbett replies that this is almost never the case. His rejoinder comes at the outset of *Some Principles of Maritime Strategy*, where he holds that naval warfare is seldom if ever decisive in itself. "Unaided," he opines, controlling the sea-lanes can only work through "a process of exhaustion" whose "effects must always be slow, and so galling both to our own commercial community and to neutrals" that political leaders often accept a substandard compromise peace rather than keep up the pressure on enemy shipping lanes—pressure that harms commerce for foe, friend, and bystander alike.[82]

J. C. Wylie expands on the idea to which Corbett alludes, pronouncing commerce warfare, or "tonnage war," a brand of "cumulative" operations. Wylie notes that military folk typically think in terms of "sequential" campaigns. "Normally," he writes, "we consider a war as a series of discrete steps or actions, with each one of this series of actions growing naturally out of, and dependent on, the one that preceded it." Each step in the sequence—usually a tactical engagement—depends on the one that came before. If any one action had turned out differently, "the sequence would have been interrupted and altered."[83]

If the stepwise approach is familiar—sequential strategies can be plotted on the map or nautical chart with continuous lines, curves, or vectors pointing toward some final objective—Wylie also divines "another way to prosecute a war." Some operations are "made up of a collection of lesser actions, but these lesser or individual actions are not sequentially interdependent. Each individual one is no more than a single statistic, an isolated plus or minus, in arriving at the final result."[84] Tactical engagements take place independently of one another and do not cascade in linear sequence toward some final objective. Plotted on the map or chart, cumulative actions appear as though a two-year-old had dipped her fingers in paint and splattered it everywhere (as mine used to do).

Prosecuted with sufficient resources, fervor, and patience, cumulative operations grind down an opponent. No engagement is decisive in itself, or even significant. Losing one freighter or transport makes little difference to the outcome of a war. Cumulatively, though, the impact of losing many freighters or transports over time could be grave. This is war by statistics, and—as Corbett notes—it works by wearying foes over time. The U.S. submarine campaign against Japan during World War II was a quintessential cumulative campaign and likely the one that inspired Wylie, a veteran of that conflict.

Like Corbett, Admiral Wylie denies that cumulative operations—surface raiding, submarine warfare, aerial bombardment, or insurgent or counterinsurgent warfare—ever decide the outcome of war in themselves.[85] At most, they could exhaust an opponent if prosecuted for a very long time. He does claim, however, that cumulative operations can make the difference between two evenly matched antagonists that deploy sequential operations against each other.[86] The paint-splatter approach makes a difference at the margins by wearing down enemy power to undertake sequential operations. If the cumulative approach is a difference-maker, it behooves maritime strategists to consider how to wage nonlinear warfare against their opponents to supplement linear campaigns—and how to counter enemy cumulative operations.

Troublemaking Strategy: War by Contingent

There are other ways to debilitate an opponent. For instance, Corbett presses strategists to figure out how to wage "war limited by contingent" against their adversaries in major wars. As a rule, political leaders and top commanders set certain operational and strategic aims for a theater of war and dispatch forces to achieve them. The goal-driven approach helps advance overall political objectives. Wars by contingent defy the rule. As the name implies, senior leaders assign a commander a contingent of forces along with instructions to open a new combat theater and make as much trouble as possible for the enemy. This is a resource-driven rather than goal-driven mode of war-making.

Great Britain deployed such a troublemaking strategy against Napoleonic France on the Iberian Peninsula. Corbett recounts how Sir Arthur Wellesley, later the Duke of Wellington and the victor of Waterloo, led a modest "disposal force" of about fifty thousand redcoats onto the peninsula in 1808. (To oversimplify, a disposal force is a force that a combatant can spare for a peripheral campaign such as Wellington's without starving the main theater or campaign of resources needed to prevail in that theater. It would make little sense to risk what policymakers hold dear for the sake of something secondary.) Supported from seaward by the Royal Navy, Wellington's army worked alongside Portuguese and Spanish partisans to bog down French forces—siphoning them away from the major fighting to France's east.[87] So effective was British and allied mischief-making that Napoleon joked ruefully about his "Spanish Ulcer."[88]

Like an ulcer, prosecuting a war by contingent inflicts nonfatal but gnawing pain that distracts its victim and never subsides. The U.S. decision to fight in the Solomon Islands after the Imperial Japanese Navy went there likewise qualifies as a war by contingent. Japan could ill afford its losses in the Solomons, while America needed somewhere to rumble in the Pacific while its armed forces mustered manpower back home and industry manufactured enough war matériel for offensive operations. Japan too suffered an ulcer. Strategic overseers should think about where and how to inflict ulcers on their adversaries—easing pressure in major theaters while sapping foes' resolve and resources.

Old Ideas Made New: Access and Area Denial

The U.S. strategic community has a penchant for slapping a new label on some old phenomenon and pronouncing that phenomenon something never seen before. For instance, scholars and press accounts hailed Gen. David Petraeus for pioneering a new counterinsurgent strategy for Iraq—never mind that he codified his supposedly new insights in a field manual strongly reminiscent of the *Small Wars Manual* published by the U.S. Marine Corps in 1940, a host of preexisting theoretical works on insurgency, and well over a century of U.S. military experience with irregular warfare.[89] This is just one example underscoring a larger American proclivity for forgetfulness.

This is a proclivity worth fighting. There is little new under the sun in martial affairs. Sea services that forget and must rediscover past wisdom hobble themselves intellectually relative to competitors who study the past and draw insight from it. The rediscovery process wastes effort and time.

A recent case in point is the debate over "access denial" and "area denial" strategy and weaponry. The concept of access denial is a hoary one, a descendant of the venerable concept of "sea denial." High technology has breathed new life into vintage strategic ideas under the aegis of access and area denial. Commonly deployed by regional antagonists today, such strategies entertain twofold aims. One, their practitioners prefer to deter external foes altogether from entering zones to which they want to bar access. They could do so by harnessing Kissinger's logic of deterrence. Demonstrating the capacity to strike effectively throughout the no-go zone—and pummel shipping that dares enter—is the goal of deterrence. If the outside power's leaders do not desire their goals enough to pay a heavy price for them, measured in damaged or sunken vessels and wounded or drowned sailors, they may desist from trying to break into the access-denial zone. Deterrence succeeds by skewing the enemy's cost-benefit calculations against intervening.

Or, two, access-denial defenses must be potent enough to carry out the deterrent threat their users have issued, slowing down an opponent who defies the threat and accepts the price of entry. Time is what the defender covets. Meting out punishment weakens the foe's fleet and could stall its advance, granting the defender enough time to accomplish its goals in the theater before the foe reaches it. Even if the antagonist belatedly breaks through anti-access defenses, the defender may have already staged a fait accompli. In other words, the home team will have created facts on the ground that the visiting team can reverse only at extreme cost and peril—if at all. Cost-benefit calculations militate against such a course of action.

Japanese strategists pioneered access denial for the air age. By 1907 the Imperial Japanese Navy designated the U.S. Navy as its next probable enemy.[90] Planners envisioned stationing warplanes on Pacific islands and submarines in adjacent waters. These forward pickets would snipe at the U.S. Pacific Fleet as it steamed from Hawaii or the American West Coast to the relief of the Philippine Islands, most likely, or of some other beleaguered territory. Japanese strategists did not delude themselves that they could win outright through piecemeal attacks. They anticipated inflicting damage and wearying the foe. Repeated pinprick strikes would even the odds between mismatched fleets as a prelude to a decisive battle somewhere in the western Pacific.

In other words, access denial constitutes a form of active defense and a weaker defender's great equalizer. It can hamper a stronger foe while hewing that foe down to size—and help the defender compete with a decent chance to prevail. Defenders can repurpose Mahan's "broad formula" for sizing fleets (reviewed in chapter 2) thus: *a battle fleet backed by shore-based firepower should be great enough to take to the sea and fight with reasonable prospects of success against the largest force it is likely to encounter.* In all likelihood, a fraction of the U.S. Navy and affiliated joint forces will face off against the whole of an antagonist's battle fleet backed by its air force and strategic missile force. An anti-access foe's joint sea, missile, and defenses constitute the measuring stick for whether U.S. and allied forces are powerful enough to achieve their goals in Eurasian waters and skies.

Access denial, in short, is not about erecting an impenetrable wall that halts all entrants.[91] Not even China's Great Wall met that standard in land warfare. The Great Wall blunted and channeled Central Asian nomads' attacks so mobile forces stationed behind the wall could meet and defeat them after they broke through, and that was the purpose its architects had in mind.[92] Access denial is about riding out the impact of an assault and keeping that assault from reaching battlegrounds the defender treasures most, deep within the no-go zone. For instance, if China's military needs a few days to conquer Taiwan and can slow down U.S. intervention for that few days or longer, then access denial will have fulfilled its goal. In football terms, access denial is a "bend but don't break" defense.[93] And it is a mode of defense that is increasingly plausible for weaker contestants looking to make things rough on stronger outsiders plying offshore waters.

In short, the idea of obstructing access is nothing new.[94] A century ago Alfred Thayer Mahan caught sight of a battle method that is coming into its own for the first time with the advent of long-range precision–guided armaments. This was the "fortress fleet," and it constitutes part of access denial.[95] Mahan decried Russian commanders' practice of keeping the bulk of the Russian Pacific Fleet under the guns of Port Arthur, the great harbor on China's Liaotung Peninsula, for protection during the Russo-Japanese War of 1904–5. Ostensibly the fleet was the fort's offshore defender; in reality it took refuge under the fort's guns. Mahan depicted operating a battle fleet as a fortress fleet as a "radically erroneous" way of doing business in great waters. Sheltering within reach of shore gunnery circumscribed fighting ships' radius of action while breeding timidity and defensive-mindedness in commanders. After all, the maximum effective firing range of a cannon in 1904–5 was a meager few miles. Tracing a circle on the map with that radius, centered on the fort, delineates the operating grounds for a fortress fleet. This is a cramped sea area indeed.

Mahan was right for his time, but his critique hinged on the state of military technology, not some flaw in the concept. Gunnery and fire control could not put the concept of long-range fire support into practice during the Russo-Japanese War. But the idea itself is sound. Try a thought experiment. What if the guns of Port Arthur had boasted sufficient range and precision to strike against Japanese shipping throughout the Yellow Sea and Tsushima Strait, where the climactic naval engagements took place? This is the proper analogy to today. Precise coastal artillery would have afforded the Russian fleet protection against Adm. Tōgō Heihachirō's superior fleet throughout the combat theater, and what would have happened is anyone's guess. Things likely would have turned out better for St. Petersburg had accurate Russian fire support extended hundreds of miles offshore rather than a scant few miles. Coastal fire would have empowered Russian commanders to pursue wide-ranging operations in offshore waters while still enjoying protective cover from the fort.

In reality, then, Mahan paid homage to the fortress-fleet concept in a backhanded way. No longer is this brand of strategy erroneous. Indeed, it is an obvious choice for local defenders. To name one, China has founded its access-denial strategy largely on its inventory of antiship and antiair missiles. The

People's Liberation Army fields a Rocket Force armed with antiship ballistic missiles reputedly able to strike at moving ships hundreds of miles offshore, well before they can close on scenes of battle to which they might be ordered. It is doubtful that Chinese strategists needed to investigate the Russo-Japanese War to get the idea for long-range fire support, but the Mahanian notion of the fortress fleet ratifies their thinking.

Nor is the fortress fleet the only old idea made new in recent years. Adm. Théophile Aube was Mahan's alter ego. The French commander was a progenitor of the "*jeune école*," a nineteenth-century school of naval strategy that sought to counter oceangoing hegemons such as Great Britain's Royal Navy. The concept envisioned a kind of near-shore guerrilla war. *Jeune école* disciples believed a second-rate naval power like Aube's France could shoo overpowering fleets away from off-shore waters by harnessing asymmetric technology manifest in torpedoes, sea mines, submarines, and surface patrol craft. Such vessels were light and inexpensive but could plague battleships and cruisers in coastal waters.[96] That was good enough for a continental power like France that merely needed to safeguard its coastal frontier. *Jeune école* craft comprised the superempowered flotilla that so vexed Corbett (see chapter 2). This was the essence of sea denial.

What was a promising idea in Admiral Aube's day resonates even more with today's realities. Technology has armed subs and surface craft with weapons capable of striking heavy blows at surface combatants—and in the process rendered *jeune école* strategies workable in a way they never were during Aube's lifetime, when torpedoes and mines remained in their infancy. Merging the *jeune école* and fortress-fleet concepts with precision technology yields a defender that deploys shore-based armaments in concert with swarms of short-range missile- and torpedo-armed craft to oppose the nautical hegemon of our age—the U.S. Navy.

And it can do so with considerable prospects of success. Anti-access augments the firepower organic to the defender's battle fleet and in turn exacts heavy costs from great-power forces that venture onto the defender's home ground. In short, shore-based sea power constitutes a lesser power's way to even the score against a stronger power fighting far from home. A fleet that is a beneficiary of shore fire support stands a chance against a stronger fleet if the fight takes place within range of that fire support—as most future fights will, judging from statements of strategic purpose issuing from Washington, Beijing, Moscow, and other potential belligerents.

Theodore Roosevelt merits the last word on combined sea- and land-based sea power. In his 1907 message to Congress, and again in an address to the 1908 "Battleship Conference" at the Naval War College, President Roosevelt held forth on the symbiosis between land and sea power. For him, these constituted mutually reinforcing arms of military might. He maintained that coastal gunners and small-ship crews should shoulder the burden of safeguarding seaports against seaborne assault. By defending the coast, they would liberate the battle fleet to carry the fight to foes cruising the high seas. A joint division of labor, in TR's words, would render the fleet "footloose," freeing it to "search out and destroy the enemy's fleet." That errand of destruction, declared the president, represents "the only function that can justify the fleet's existence."[97]

Like TR's coastal artillery and light warships, a sufficiently dense thicket of offshore defenses could render surface fleets footloose today. And that is the ultimate goal of those making these old strategic ideas new. Local great powers could shield their homelands and nearby expanses mainly with fortress-fleet and *jeune école* platforms—freeing up the bulk of their surface fleets for expeditionary ventures in distant waters. Sea power is no longer a matter for fighting ships alone. It is a matter for joint forces able to project power to contested zones on the map. Strategists must likewise think jointly.[98]

A Machiavellian Warning: Tend the Culture

Strategists and sea services must master all of the concepts and ideas presented in this volume and more. Niccolò Machiavelli would add that girding for future combat is a cultural project as much as a matter of devising new technology and inventive ways to use it to fulfill operational and strategic aims. It is about refreshing sea-service culture for new times. This is a never-ending task; the times are always new! In parting, consequently, it is worth recalling Admiral Mahan's admonition that maritime strategy never ceases. Officialdom must prosecute it in wartime and peacetime alike. In peacetime strategists' job is to amass and husband the trappings of sea power—initiating and sustaining the virtuous cycle among commerce, diplomacy, and naval might.

In the naval and military realm, that involves building and maintaining equipment and weapons, administering programs, and executing the myriad other tasks that consume daily life in armed services. They must keep the "supply chain" for naval power unbroken and strong (see chapters 1 and 2). And it involves honing human excellence with the same determination and zeal that professionals bring to the material dimension of strategy and operations. Nourishing an institutional culture that favors peacetime and especially wartime supremacy is crucial to competing and prevailing in warlike endeavors.

A comprehensive treatment of institutional culture is beyond the scope of this short book, but leaders at all levels should take a few pointers from the masters to heart. They should take inspiration from Machiavelli's insights into human nature, the ordeal of change, and the imperative to surmount that ordeal in order to flourish. First and foremost, orthodoxy is the death of entrepreneurship. Sociologist Max Weber portrays bureaucratic institutions like navies, armies, and air forces as machines.[99] Standard rules and procedures govern operations.

And that was a good thing from Weber's standpoint a century ago. Much like physical machinery, a bureaucracy executes the same routine tasks over and over again, exactly the same way each time. It performs a standard repertoire with machine-like efficiency. Accordingly, bureaucratic practice rewards those who carry out routine chores efficiently while punishing those who do not. Promotions, awards, and bonuses go to smoothly functioning cogs in the works.

But think about it. Machinery has worked wonders for modern civilization, but machines do not readily reinvent themselves for tasks outside their repertoire, let alone adapt easily when the operating environment changes around them. Robert Komer, who served alongside U.S. Army forces in Vietnam while presiding over a civil-military command, contends that the world wars and Korean War forged the Army's way of war. Army officers had grown accustomed to fighting on conventional battlegrounds. Conventional warfare was baked into Army doctrine and hardware as a result. Soldiers deployed to Indochina expecting to fight a conventional war, and that was what they set about doing.[100] Retired Army officer Andrew Krepinevich agrees that the service projected the generals' fixed "concept" of war onto the Vietnam War—and tried to fit the reality of insurgent warfare to its preexisting preferences.[101]

Reality refused to comply with Army preconceptions. The bureaucratic machinery tried to do what the leadership had programmed it to do, and the results disappointed. Nor are navies exempt from this malady. All big organizations are prone to set and enforce orthodox views and practices. How can naval leaders escape this tendency? By understanding that it exists, for one thing. The first step toward solving a problem is admitting there is a problem. By finding, appointing, and empowering "devil's advocates," for another. The medieval church designated a lawyer to contest the qualifications of any candidate for sainthood, arguing against the candidate's credentials by means fair or foul. Church fathers solicited the best arguments against canonization. Having the full range of pros and cons before them sharpened their thinking, counteracted orthodoxy, and bolstered the likelihood of a sound decision.

Research psychologist Irving Janis updates the concept of the devil's advocate for modern times and prescribes it as an organization's best antidote to "groupthink." Groupthink is a process whereby groups bring pressure on dissenters from some idea or proposed course of action. Social pressure induces dissidents to agree with the group or remain silent. It stymies creativity. To combat groupthink Janis beseeches leaders to add a freethinker to every team and to make that person's evaluations and career rewards contingent on combating conventional wisdom with ingenuity and aplomb.[102] Wise naval leaders will heed Janis' counsel.

Second, abjure truisms. All doctrine should be tentative and treated as subject to change with the times and surroundings. As pointed out before, Julian Corbett made sport of the "battle faith" that gripped the Royal Navy leadership of his day. Nothing, he insisted, is "so dangerous in the study of war as to permit maxims to become a substitute for judgment."[103] Nor is thinking in truisms a peculiarly British problem. Bernard Brodie, one of the great American strategists of the twentieth century, contends that a tyranny of maxims enslaved military minds throughout the West in the years before World War I. French generals, to name just one example, talked themselves into believing they could array "men against fire"—that is, infantrymen against fixed fortifications—and prevail if there was adequate fighting spirit in the ranks.[104] The repercussions proved disastrous. Naval leaders must guard against the tendency to think in truisms, maxims, or creeds. It can disarm their critical faculties. Believing in fixed truths about the naval profession inhibits adaptation to stay abreast of changing times. It could deform the making and execution of maritime strategy.

Third, beware the pitfalls of winning too big in war. A transcendent victory deprives the victor of an enemy and, thus, of the incentive to stay sharp in intellectual and material terms. As the Anglo-Irish parliamentarian Edmund Burke noted in 1790: "Difficulty is a severe instructor. . . . He that wrestles with us strengthens our nerves and sharpens our skill. Our antagonist is our helper. This amicable conflict with difficulty obliges us to an intimate acquaintance with our object and compels us to consider it in all its relations. It will not suffer us to be superficial."[105]

Just so. Historian Andrew Gordon chronicles how the Royal Navy won a smashing triumph at the Battle of Trafalgar in 1805, crushing its principal foe, a Franco-Spanish maritime alliance. No one posed a formidable challenge to British maritime mastery for the balance of the nineteenth century, and the Royal Navy spent its time fighting outmatched opponents in imperial police actions. Trafalgar had perverse fallout in that it eliminated the likeliest peer enemy, the French navy, and in the process denied naval chieftains a focal point for thinking about strategy, operations, and fleet design. Royal Navy leaders succumbed to vices with no peer enemy to keep them on their toes. They yielded to the temptation to centralize control of tactics and administrative affairs. Senior leadership took to choreographing fleet maneuvers and other endeavors in minute detail. Instead of granting ship captains and more junior sailors the latitude to handle their ships with panache, thereby unlocking their creative energies, top commanders stifled entrepreneurship within the officer corps.

In short, the devil-may-care Royal Navy of Horatio Nelson's day metamorphosed into a force of control freaks whose excesses left the navy ill prepared for the challenge it would confront in the form of an enterprising German High Seas Fleet after the turn of the twentieth century. Bad habits worked against British tactical acumen at the Battle of Jutland (1916) and other engagements.[106]

Gordon labels the aftermath of Trafalgar the "long calm lee" of a stunning triumph.[107] His metaphor is well chosen. The lee is the downwind side of some object, whether a ship, a landmass, or something else. The bulk of that object blocks out the wind and the elements, making the weather seem more tranquil than it is outside that refuge. The lee shelters refugees from reality for a time. A *long* lee might delude its beneficiaries into believing the weather is always calm. Mariners plying placid waters lose the seamanship and mental edge needed to cope with sea and sky in all their fury.

A Trafalgar has that effect. By eradicating threats for a long time, a major triumph seduces service chieftains and officialdom into believing the next peer competitor or climactic battle will never come along. And if not, why waste effort and finite resources preparing for one? A long calm lee has beguiled the U.S. Navy into complacency on occasion. Harvard professor Samuel Huntington notes that sinking Axis navies in World War II left the service strategically rudderless. Its vast armada floated "in solitary splendor" for no apparent reason now that its enemies littered the bottom of the oceans. The navy needed a strategic concept to justify its existence before Congress and to guide thinking about future contingencies.[108]

More recently the naval leadership issued a directive titled " . . . From the Sea: Preparing the Naval Service for the 21st Century" (1992) in an effort to sculpt strategy for the post–Cold War era. The leadership proclaimed, without quite saying so, that naval history had ended.[109] With no Soviet Navy left to fight and no new rival on the horizon, the U.S. Navy and Marine Corps could afford to transform themselves into a "fundamentally different naval force."[110] They could assume no one would dispute American command of the sea. The sea was now an offshore sanctuary from which U.S. expeditionary forces could project power ashore, render humanitarian assistance, and conduct other worthwhile missions. Battle was passé.

In other words, " . . . From the Sea" declared that U.S. and allied forces could exploit command of the sea without fighting for it. The end of history had repealed their first and most vital mission: preparing for or waging major battle. Having received a powerful mandate from on high, the naval services set about executing it. Education, training, and hardware necessary for combat against peer navies languished in the long calm lee of the Cold War.

A false calm masks reality. Reality has a way of reasserting itself with sudden force when the calm passes. Abrupt change disorients those exposed to the weather anew. The U.S. sea services have emerged from the post–Cold War lull and find themselves struggling to cope with history's return. The elements now buffet them in the form of great-power competition from China, Russia, and other aspirants to regional or world power.

The sea services could have avoided such travails had they kept a tragic view of their profession. It is natural to welcome a pause from great-power competition, but warriors should never kid themselves that it has ceased forever. A new competitor will always come along sooner or later, and competition will resume. This is in the nature of things. Service leaders are now attempting to overhaul U.S. naval culture along with the fleet. By no means is success a foregone conclusion. It's one thing to bask in the afterglow of victory—quite another to declare that victory is forever.

Lastly, and above all, a healthy institutional culture rejects hubris. The ancients warned against this outrageous form of arrogance. It brought on punishment from the gods, or Fate, or Providence.[111] Pride goes before a fall, as the proverb puts it. It is all too easy for a force that has reigned supreme for years or decades to believe supremacy is a birthright, and to disparage new challengers. Across the decades, for example, the U.S. Navy has congratulated itself on its foresight during wargames at the Naval War College in the 1920s and 1930s. A post–World War II quotation from Adm. Chester Nimitz commonly makes the rounds, crediting the college with foreseeing everything that transpired in the Pacific theater except for Japanese kamikazes.[112]

And the interwar generation does deserve plaudits. Still, the service fell prey to hubris vis-à-vis the Imperial Japanese Navy in important respects. Naval officers found it unfathomable that Japanese weapons engineers could improvise a torpedo able to strike capital ships in the shallow basin of Pearl Harbor. And yet they did, in the form of the Long Lance torpedo.

Why deprecate a formidable antagonist? Novelist Ernest Hemingway maintains that the U.S. Navy forgot how the Japanese Combined Fleet had annihilated the Russian Baltic Fleet at Tsushima Strait in 1905, spelling an end to Russian naval power in the Far East until the Soviet Navy's renaissance during the Cold War. Prevailing opinion held that the Japanese Empire was a "great pushover." "One cruiser division and a couple of carriers would destroy Tokyo" once battle was joined, as Hemingway sums up the mentality; "another ditto Yokohama."[113]

No one truly imagined that the Japanese might take matters into their own hands—and unleash a Pearl Harbor. In other words, hubris tinged even impressive efforts to glimpse the future and prepare for it. Studying strategy and history throughout a career in uniform—not just when assigned to the schoolhouse—will inoculate seafarers and the service as a whole against taking tough rivals lightly. Affording them respect constitutes the beginning of strategic wisdom. Maritime strategy is apt to falter without it.

Notes

Preface

1. Former secretary of the Navy John Lehman relays the quotation. John F. Lehman, *Command of the Seas* (1988; repr., Annapolis, Md.: Naval Institute Press, 2001), 25.
2. Hughes' treatise is now in its third edition. Wayne Hughes, *Fleet Tactics and Naval Operations*, 3rd ed. (Annapolis, Md.: Naval Institute Press, 2018).
3. John B. Hattendorf and Lynn C. Hattendorf, *A Bibliography of the Works of Alfred Thayer Mahan* (Newport, R.I.: Naval War College Press, 1986).
4. Carl von Clausewitz, *On War*, trans. Michael Howard and Peter Paret (Princeton, N.J.: Princeton University Press, 1976), 141.
5. Clausewitz, 141.

Chapter 1. How to Generate Sea Power

1. Probably the best biography of Mahan comes from Robert Seager, who also coedited his letters and papers. See Robert Seager II, *Alfred Thayer Mahan: The Man and His Letters* (Annapolis, Md.: Naval Institute Press, 1977).
2. Such religious imagery is commonplace when discussing Mahan, who hoped to summon forth American society's seafaring spirit. He was dubbed an evangelist and a Copernicus among many other monikers. Margaret Sprout, "Mahan: Evangelist of Sea Power," in *Makers of Modern Strategy*, ed. Edward Mead Earle (Princeton, N.J.: Princeton University Press, 1986), 415–45.
3. Alfred Thayer Mahan, *The Influence of Sea Power upon History, 1660–1783* (1890; repr., New York: Dover, 1987), 138.
4. Alfred Thayer Mahan, *The Problem of Asia* (Boston: Little, Brown, 1900), 29–30, 33.
5. Alfred Thayer Mahan, *Retrospect & Prospect: Studies in International Relations, Naval and Political* (Boston: Little, Brown, 1902), 246.
6. Mahan, 246.
7. Mahan, 246.
8. Robert B. Strassler, ed., *The Landmark Thucydides*, intro. Victor Davis Hanson (New York: Touchstone, 1996), 46.

9. Strassler, 81–82.

10. Mahan, *Influence of Sea Power upon History*, 25, 138.

11. "A Tour of New England's Uncommon Town Commons," New England Historical Society, accessed July 10, 2018, http://www.newenglandhistoricalsociety .com/tour-new-englands-uncommon-town-commons/.

12. Max Weber, *Politics as a Vocation* (New York: Oxford University Press, 1946), 3.

13. Hugo Grotius, *The Freedom of the Seas*, trans. Ralph Van Deman Magoffin, intro. James Brown Scott (New York: Oxford University Press, 1916).

14. John Selden, *On the Dominion, Or, Ownership of the Sea, Two Books* (London: Council of State, 1652), https://archive.org/details/ofdominionorowne00seld. The quotation comes from the cover page of the book and has been updated slightly for modern readers.

15. "President Woodrow Wilson's Fourteen Points," January 8, 1918, Yale Law School Avalon Project Web site, http://avalon.law.yale .edu/20th_Century/wilson14.asp. For an exhaustive look at the topic, see James Kraska and Raul Pedrozo, *The Free Sea: The American Fight for Freedom of Navigation* (Annapolis, Md.: Naval Institute Press, 2018).

16. Tommy T. B. Koh, "A Constitution for the Oceans," UN Web site, https://www.un.org/Depts/los/convention_agreements/texts/koh_english.pdf. The full text of the law of the sea—must reading for any maritime strategist—is found on the UN Web site at https://www.un.org/Depts/los/convention_agreements/texts/unclos/closindx.htm. The ensuing discussion of the convention draws on this text.

17. UN Convention on the Law of the Sea, UN Web site, https://www.un.org/Depts/los/convention_agreements/texts/unclos/closindx.htm.

18. International Maritime Organization, "Convention for the Suppression of Unlawful Acts Against the Safety of Maritime Navigation, Protocol for the Suppression of Unlawful Acts Against the Safety of Fixed Platforms Located on the Continental Shelf," IMO Web site, accessed July 10, 2018, http://www.imo.org/en/About/Conventions/ListOfConventions/Pages/SUA-Treaties.aspx.

19. U.S. State Department, "Maritime Security and Navigation," U.S. State Department Website, https://www.state.gov/e/oes/ocns/opa/maritimesecurity/.

20. People's Republic of China, "CML/17/2009," document submitted by the People's Republic of China to the United Nations Commission on the Limits of the Continental Shelf, May 7, 2009, UN Web site, http://www.un.org/depts/los/clcs_new/submissions_files/mysvnm33_09/chn_2009re_mys_vnm_e.pdf; and John Pomfret, "Beijing Claims 'Indisputable Sovereignty' over South China Sea," *Washington Post*, July 31, 2010, http://www.washingtonpost.com/wp-dyn/content/article/2010/07/30/AR2010073005664.html?noredirect=on. See also "China Deploys Missiles in South China Sea, Says It Has 'Indisputable Sovereignty,'" *Times of India*, May 3, 2018, http://timesofindia.indiatimes.com/articleshow/64016130.cms?utm_source=contentofinterest&utm_medium=text&utm_campaign=cppst. The language mariners use to describe their endeavors is important.

Chinese officialdom hastens to assure seafaring governments that it has no desire to interfere with "freedom of navigation." But Beijing interprets freedom of navigation as the freedom to pass through regional waters—and do nothing else while in transit. In other words, it insists that shipping comply with the rules of innocent passage. Mariners should stress that their governments abide by the doctrine of freedom of the sea and insist on all of their rights under UNCLOS.

21. Dexter Perkins, *A History of the Monroe Doctrine* (Boston: Little, Brown, 1963).

22. Article 21 acknowledges the Monroe Doctrine. "Treaty of Peace with Germany (Treaty of Versailles)," 1919, Library of Congress Web site, https://www.loc.gov/law/help/us-treaties/bevans/m-ust000002-0043.pdf.

23. Geoffrey Till, *Seapower*, 3rd ed. (London: Routledge, 2013), 5–22.

24. Till, 14–17.

25. Edward N. Luttwak, *The Political Uses of Sea Power* (Baltimore: Johns Hopkins University Press, 1974), 6, 11, 14–15.

26. Koh, "A Constitution for the Oceans."

27. UN Convention on the Law of the Sea, parts V and XI, UN Web site, http://www.un.org/Depts/los/convention_agreements/texts/ unclos/closindx.htm.

28. See, for instance, Peter J. Dutton, "Carving Up the East China Sea," *Naval War College Review* 60, no. 2 (Spring 2007): 45–68.

29. Till, *Seapower*, 282–317.

30. Robert D. Kaplan, *Monsoon: The Indian Ocean and the Future of American Power* (New York: Random House, 2011).

31. The name dates to the nineteenth century but has taken on new currency with the rise of China and India to maritime power. Rory Medcalf, "The Indo-Pacific: What's in a Name?" *American Interest* 9, no. 2 (October 10, 2013), https://www.the-american-interest.com/2013/10/10/the-indo-pacific-whats -in-a-name/.

32. Alfred Thayer Mahan, *The Gulf and Inland Waters* (New York: Scribner, 1883).

33. Kemp Tolley, *Yangtze Patrol: The U.S. Navy in China* (Annapolis, Md.: Naval Institute Press, 1971).

34. Mahan, *Influence of Sea Power upon History*, 44.

35. Mahan, 44.

36. James Stavridis, *Sea Power: The History and Geopolitics of the World's Oceans* (New York: Penguin, 2017), 4.

37. James R. Holmes, "I Served Aboard One of the Last U.S. Navy Battleships. And It Changed My Life," *National Interest*, June 22, 2018, https://nationalinterest .org/blog/the-buzz/i-served-aboard-one-the-last-us-navy-battleships-it -changed-26392.

38. Stavridis, *Sea Power*, 4.

39. Alfred Thayer Mahan, *The Interest of America in Sea Power, Present and Future* (Boston: Little, Brown, 1897), 41–42.

40. "Navigational Mathematics," American Mathematical Society Web site, accessed June 28, 2018, http://www.ams.org/publicoutreach/feature-column/

fcarc-navigation3. For much more, see Thomas J. Cutler, *Dutton's Nautical Navigation*, 15th ed. (Annapolis, Md.: Naval Institute Press, 2003).

41. Julian S. Corbett, *Some Principles of Maritime Strategy* (1911; repr., Annapolis, Md.: Naval Institute Press, 1988), 262–79.

42. Alfred Thayer Mahan, *The Influence of Sea Power upon the French Revolution and Empire* (Boston: Little, Brown, 1892), 1:123.

43. Corbett, *Some Principles of Maritime Strategy*, 106, 261–65, 276.

44. Krishnadev Calamur, "High Traffic, High Risk in the Strait of Malacca," *Atlantic*, August 21, 2017, https://www.theatlantic.com/international/archive/2017/08/strait-of-malacca-uss-john-mccain/537471/.

45. Mahan, *Interest of America in Sea Power*, 41–42.

46. "The Lighthouse Joke," U.S. Navy Web site, September 2, 2009, http://www.navy.mil/navydata/nav_legacy.asp?id=174.

47. Alfred Thayer Mahan, *Naval Strategy Compared and Contrasted with the Principles and Practice of Military Operations on Land* (Boston: Little, Brown, 1911), 309–10.

48. Mahan, 309–10.

49. Mahan, 309–10.

50. See, for instance, Craig L. Symonds, *World War II at Sea* (Oxford: Oxford University Press, 2018), 403–68.

51. Mahan, *Naval Strategy*, 309–10.

52. Plato, "Apology," trans. Benjamin Jowett, Gutenberg Project, https://ia800401.us.archive.org/0/items/Apology-Socrates/Apology.pdf.

53. J. C. Wylie, *Military Strategy: A General Theory of Power Control* (1967; repr., Annapolis, Md.: Naval Institute Press, 1989), 32.

54. Alfred Thayer Mahan, "The Persian Gulf and International Relations," in Mahan, *Retrospect & Prospect*, 237.

55. Mahan, *Influence of Sea Power upon History*, 70–71.

56. Mahan, *Problem of Asia*, 26, 124.

57. The prominent British historian John Keegan, among others, testified to the impact of Mahan's writings. John Keegan, *The American Civil War* (New York: Knopf, 2009), 272. Mahan's discussion of the six determinants is found in Mahan, *Influence of Sea Power upon History*, 25–89.

58. Mahan, *Influence of Sea Power upon History*, 23.

59. Mahan, 22–23, 29.

60. George W. Baer, *One Hundred Years of Sea Power: The U.S. Navy, 1890–1990* (Stanford, Calif.: Stanford University Press, 1994), 135, 152.

61. "Oregon II (Battleship No. 3)," Naval History and Heritage Command Web site, November 9, 2016, https://www.history.navy.mil/research/histories/ship-histories/danfs/o/oregon-ii.html.

62. This was part of the premise of the 2015 novel *Ghost Fleet*. China launched an all-out assault on Oahu, Hawaii, deliberately wrecking a freighter in the Panama Canal to inhibit U.S. Navy reinforcements in the Atlantic from steaming to the Pacific Fleet's relief. Nor is this some fanciful scenario.

Navy aircraft carrier task forces have practiced raiding the canal since the 1920s. P. W. Singer and August Cole, *Ghost Fleet* (Boston: Houghton Mifflin Harcourt, 2015), 55–57, 135. See also "USS *Saratoga* (CV 3)," U.S. Navy Web site, June 11, 2009, http://www.navy.mil/navydata/nav_legacy .asp?id=12.

63. A team from the Center for Naval Analyses posits that the U.S. Navy is hovering near a "tipping point" beyond which it will no longer be a global force. Too few vessels, aircraft, and armaments will make up the inventory to discharge the missions entrusted to it. Daniel Whiteneck, Michael Price, Neil Jenkins, and Peter Swartz, *The Navy at a Tipping Point: Maritime Dominance at Stake?* (Washington, D.C.: Center for Naval Analyses, March 2010).

64. Mahan, *Influence of Sea Power upon History*, 31–32.

65. For an exhaustive look at Chinese economic and strategic geography, see Toshi Yoshihara and James R. Holmes, *Red Star over the Pacific*, 2nd ed. (Annapolis, Md.: Naval Institute Press, 2018), esp. chapters 2 and 3.

66. Mahan, *Influence of Sea Power upon History*, 33.

67. Mahan, 35.

68. Mahan, 35.

69. Mahan, 35–36.

70. Mahan, 39–40.

71. For much more on "strategic culture," a phrase coined long after the day of Mahan, see Colin S. Gray, *Out of the Wilderness: Prime Time for Strategic Culture*, October 31, 2006, Federation of American Scientists Web site, https:// fas.org/irp/agency/dod/dtra/stratcult-out.pdf. Scholar Charles Kupchan defines strategic culture as "the realm of national identity and national self-image." It consists of "images and symbols that shape how a polity understands its relationship between metropolitan security and empire, conceives of its position in the international hierarchy, and perceives the nature and scope of the nation's external ambition. These images and symbols at once *mold public attitudes and become institutionalized and routinized in the structure and process of decision making*. . . . Inasmuch as strategic culture shapes the boundaries of politically legitimate behavior in the realm of foreign policy and affects how elites conceive of the national interest and set strategic priorities, it plays a *crucial role in shaping grand strategy*." Charles Kupchan, *The Vulnerability of Empire* (Ithaca, N.Y.: Cornell University Press, 1994), 5–6; my emphasis. In short, history and traditions bequeathed from generation to generation shape the worldviews, habits of mind, and actions of strategic elites and ordinary folk in a society.

72. Mahan, *Influence of Sea Power upon History*, 37.

73. Mahan, 36–37.

74. Jeremy Black, "A British View of the Naval War of 1812," *Naval History* 22, no. 4 (August 2008), https://www.usni.org/magazines/navalhistory/2008-08 /british-view-naval-war-1812.

75. Mahan, *Influence of Sea Power upon History*, 43.

76. Mahan, 45.
77. Mahan, 46.
78. Mahan, 49.
79. Mahan, 53.
80. Mahan, 50.
81. Mahan, 50.
82. Mahan, 50–52.
83. Mahan, 55.
84. Mahan, 55.
85. Mahan, 53–55.
86. Mahan, 55–56.
87. Walter A. McDougall, *Promised Land, Crusader State: The American Encounter with the World since 1776* (Boston: Houghton Mifflin, 1997), 8.
88. Mahan, *Influence of Sea Power upon History*, 55, 56.
89. Mahan, 83.
90. Suzanne Geisler, *God and Sea Power: The Influence of Religion on Alfred Thayer Mahan* (Annapolis, Md.: Naval Institute Press, 2015), 134–35.
91. See, for instance, Butch Bracknell and James Kraska, "Ending America's 'Sea Blindness,'" *Baltimore Sun*, December 6, 2010, http://articles.baltimoresun.com/2010-12-06/news/bs-ed-sea-treaty-20101206_1_negotiation-strategic-security-american-security.
92. Mahan, *Influence of Sea Power upon the French Revolution and Empire*, 1:118.
93. Mahan retired as a captain but was advanced to rear admiral on the retired list in 1906.
94. Mahan, *Influence of Sea Power upon History*, 82.
95. Mahan, 82.
96. Mahan, 58.
97. Mahan, 58–59.
98. Mahan, 70.
99. Mahan, 69–72.
100. Mahan, 71.
101. Mahan, 71–73.
102. Mahan, 68.
103. Mahan, 68–69.
104. Mahan, 58.
105. Mahan, 62.
106. Wolfgang Wegener, *The Naval Strategy of the World War* (1929; repr., Annapolis, Md.: Naval Institute Press, 1989), 95.
107. Wegener, 96.
108. Mahan, *Influence of Sea Power upon History*, 63.
109. Mahan, 505–42.
110. Mahan, 67.
111. Mahan, 67.
112. Mahan, 67.

Chapter 2. How to Keep the Virtuous Cycle Turning

1. Alfred Thayer Mahan, *The Influence of Sea Power upon History 1660–1783* (1890; repr., New York: Dover, 1987), 70–71.

2. Mahan, 70–71.

3. "MCPON Visits United States Naval Academy," U.S. Navy Website, March 1, 2012, http://www.navy.mil/submit/display .asp?story_id=65648.

4. Mahan, *Influence of Sea Power upon History*, 28.

5. Mahan, 28.

6. Jean-Paul Rodrigue, "The Geography of Global Supply Chains," *Journal of Supply Chain Management* 48, no. 3 (July 2012): 15–23. See also John-Paul Rodrigue, ed., *The Geography of Transport Systems*, 4th ed. (London: Routledge, 2017).

7. Evidently this is a case of minds running in parallel, as Rodrigue reports being unfamiliar with Mahan's writings. Exchange of correspondence between the author and Jean-Paul Rodrigue, July 31, 2018.

8. Edward N. Luttwak, "From Geopolitics to Geoeconomics: Logic of Conflict, Grammar of Commerce," *National Interest* 20 (Summer 1990): 17–23.

9. For much more, see Toshi Yoshihara and James R. Holmes, *Red Star over the Pacific: China's Rise and the Challenge to U.S. Military Strategy*, 2nd ed. (Annapolis, Md.: Naval Institute Press, 2018), esp. chap. 2, "Economic Geography of Chinese Sea Power."

10. Yoshihara and Holmes, esp. chap. 3, "Strategic Geography of Chinese Sea Power."

11. Bradley A. Fiske, *The Navy as a Fighting Machine*, intro. Wayne P. Hughes Jr. (1916; repr., Annapolis, Md.: Naval Institute Press, 1988), 268.

12. George W. Baer, *One Hundred Years of Sea Power: The U.S. Navy, 1890–1990* (Stanford, Calif.: Stanford University Press, 1994), 236.

13. Fiske, *Navy as a Fighting Machine*, 269.

14. Two sub tenders remain in commission while all destroyer tenders have been retired. "United States Navy Fact File: Submarine Tender (AS)," U.S. Navy Web site, November 20, 2018, https://www .navy.mil/navydata/fact_display .asp?cid=4625&tid=300&ct=4.

15. Franklin D. Roosevelt, "February 23, 1942: Fireside Chat 20: On the Progress of the War," University of Virginia Miller Center Web site, accessed July 21, 2018, https://millercenter.org/the-presidency/presidential-speeches/february-23 -1942-fire-side-chat-20-progress-war.

16. Nicholas J. Spykman, *The Geography of the Peace*, ed. Helen R. Nicholl, intro. Frederick Sherwood Dunn (New York: Harcourt, Brace, 1943), 8–18.

17. Alan K. Henrikson, "The Geographical 'Mental Maps' of American Foreign Policy Makers," *International Political Science Review* 1, no. 4 (1980): 498.

18. Alan K. Henrikson, "The Map as an 'Idea': The Role of Cartographic Imagery during the Second World War," *American Cartographer* 2, no. 1 (1975): 19–53.

19. Henrikson, "Geographical 'Mental Maps,'" 498–99.

20. Henrikson, 498.

21. C. Raja Mohan, "India and the Balance of Power," *Foreign Affairs*, July/August 2006, https://www.foreignaffairs.com/articles/asia/ 2006-07-01/india-and -balance-power.

22. Yoshihara and Holmes, *Red Star over the Pacific*, esp. chap. 2 and 3.

23. J. C. Wylie, *Military Strategy: A General Theory of Power Control* (1967; repr., Annapolis, Md.: Naval Institute Press, 1989), 32–48.

24. Henrikson, "The Map as an 'Idea,'" 19.

25. Hillary Clinton, "America's Pacific Century," *Foreign Policy*, October 11, 2011, https://foreignpolicy.com/2011/10/11/americas-pacific-century/;U.S. Department of Defense, *Sustaining Global Leadership: Priorities for 21st Century Defense*, January 2012, https://archive.defense.gov/news/Defense_Strategic _Guidance.pdf; and Yuki Tatsumi, Ely Ratner, Shogo Suzuki, Edward Luttwak, Wu Jianmin, and Daniel Blumenthal, "Pivot to Asia: 'Why Keep up the Charade?'" *Foreign Policy*, April 22, 2014, https://foreignpolicy.com/2014/04/22/ pivot-to-asia-why-keep-up-the-charade/.

26. Spykman, *Geography of the Peace*, 16.

27. Darrell Huff, *How to Lie with Statistics* (New York: Norton, 1954).

28. Alfred Thayer Mahan, *Naval Strategy Compared and Contrasted with the Principles and Practice of Military Operations on Land* (Boston: Little, Brown, 1911), 319.

29. John R. Elwood, "Dennis Hart Mahan (1802–1871) and His Influence on West Point," December 6, 1995, West Point Web site, http://digital-library .usma.edu/cdm/ref/collection/p16919coll1/id/20.

30. Mahan, *Naval Strategy*, 107.

31. See, for instance, Brian R. Sullivan, "Mahan's Blindness and Brilliance," *Joint Force Quarterly* 21 (Spring 1999): 115; and J. Mohan Malik, "The Evolution of Strategic Thought," in *Contemporary Security and Strategy*, ed. Craig A. Snyder (New York: Routledge, 1999), 36.

32. Christopher Bassford, "Jomini and Clausewitz: Their Interaction," edited version of a paper presented at 23rd Meeting of the Consortium on Revolutionary Europe, Georgia State University, Atlanta, February 26, 1993, https://www.clausewitz.com/readings/Bassford/Jomini/JOMINIX.htm.

33. Spykman's term for the intermediate zones separating the "heartland," or a continent's deep interior, from the sea. Managing events in the rimlands to prevent any hostile power or coalition from constituting a threat to North America was an abiding concern for officials and geopolitics experts from the Spanish-American War forward, as the United States emerged from its century of relative seclusion from world politics.

34. Michael J. Green, *By More Than Providence: Grand Strategy and American Power in the Asia Pacific Since 1783* (New York: Columbia University Press, 2017), 87.

35. Mahan, *Influence of Sea Power upon History*, 83.

36. "Treaty of Peace between the United States and Spain; December 10, 1898," Yale University Avalon Project Web site, accessed July 21, 2018, http://avalon.law.yale.edu/19th_century/sp1898.asp.

37. Samuel Flagg Bemis, *A Diplomatic History of the United States* (New York: Henry Holt, 1942), 399, 461–62.

38. Bemis, 508–11.

39. Alfred Thayer Mahan, *The Gulf and Inland Waters* (New York: Scribner, 1883), esp. 1–8; and Philip A. Crowl, "Alfred Thayer Mahan: The Naval Historian," in *Makers of Modern Strategy from Machiavelli to the Nuclear Age*, ed. Peter Paret (Princeton, N.J.: Princeton University Press, 1986), 446.

40. Elting Morison, ed., *Letters of Theodore Roosevelt*, vol. 2 (Cambridge, Mass.: Harvard University Press, 1951), 1276–78.

41. Alfred Thayer Mahan, *The Interest of America in Sea Power, Present and Future* (Boston: Little, Brown, 1897), 39–40.

42. Mahan, 39–40.

43. Mahan, *Naval Strategy*, 132.

44. Mahan, 346.

45. Mahan, *Interest of America in Sea Power*, 41.

46. Mahan, 41.

47. Mahan, 42–45.

48. Mahan, *Naval Strategy*, 111.

49. Alfred Thayer Mahan, "The Isthmus and Sea Power," in Mahan, *Interest of America in Sea Power*, 65–68.

50. "From the King," letter from George III to Lord Sandwich, September 13, 1779, in *The Private Papers of John, Earl of Sandwich*, ed. G. R. Barnes and J. H. Owen, vol. 3 (London: Navy Records Society, 1936), 163–64.

51. Mahan, "Isthmus and Sea Power," 67–68.

52. Mahan, 78–83.

53. Spykman made the allusion between the Caribbean and Mediterranean seas explicit. Nicholas J. Spykman, *America's Strategy in World Politics: The United States and the Balance of Power* (Piscataway: Transaction, 1942), 43–95.

54. Howard K. Beale, *Theodore Roosevelt and the Rise of America to World Power* (Baltimore: Johns Hopkins University Press, 1956).

55. Spykman, *Geography of the Peace*, 23–24.

56. Spykman, 23–24.

57. Mahan, *Interest of America in Sea Power*, 275, 380.

58. Bemis, *Diplomatic History of the United States*, 511.

59. Mahan, *Naval Strategy*, 380–82.

60. Mahan, 380–82.

61. Mahan, *Interest of America in Sea Power*, 288–92.

62. Mahan, *Influence of Sea Power upon History*, 539.

63. Mahan, 539. It is commonplace for even expert commentators to claim that Mahan sets himself absolutely and resolutely against *guerre de course*. It is

worth pointing out that he saves this criticism for a footnote on the last page of *The Influence of Sea Power upon History*—and even then he concedes it is important, just not a war-winning strategy in itself.

64. For more on Confederate *guerre de course*, see Tom Chaffin, *Sea of Gray: The Around-the-World Odyssey of the Confederate Raider Shenandoah* (New York: Hill & Wang, 2006).

65. Craig Symonds, *World War II at Sea* (Oxford: Oxford University Press, 2018), 593–94; and James R. Holmes, "Where Have All the Mush Mortons Gone?" U.S. Naval Institute *Proceedings* 135, no. 6 (June 2009): 58–63.

66. Stephen Rosen, *Winning the Next War: Innovation and the Modern Military* (Ithaca, N.Y.: Cornell University Press, 1991), 130–47.

67. Garrett Mattingly, *The Armada* (Boston: Houghton Mifflin, 1959), xiv–xvi. See also "The Course of the Armada and Events in the Channel," BBC Web site, accessed July 23, 2018, https://www .bbc.com/education/guides/ z2hbtv4/revision/2.

68. "U.S.-Flag Vessels—MARAD—Maritime Administration," March 20, 2017, Maritime Administration Web site, https://www.maritime.dot .gov/sites/marad.dot.gov/files/docs/commercial-sealift/2846/dsusflag-fleet 20180301.pdf.

69. Mahan, *Interest of America in Sea Power*, 198.

70. See, for instance, Mick Ryan, *Human–Machine Teaming for Future Ground Forces* (Washington, DC: Center for Strategic and Budgetary Assessments, 2018), https://csbaonline.org/uploads/documents/Human_Machine_Teaming _FinalFormat.pdf.

71. Julian S. Corbett, *Some Principles of Maritime Strategy* (1911; repr., Annapolis, Md.: Naval Institute Press, 1988), 107.

72. Corbett, 107.

73. Corbett, 115.

74. Corbett, 114.

75. Corbett, 124, 126.

76. James R. Holmes and Toshi Yoshihara, "Garbage In, Garbage Out," *Diplomat*, January 6, 2011, https://thediplomat.com/2011/01/garbage-in -garbage-out/.

77. Mahan, *Interest of America in Sea Power*, 198.

78. For much more, see James R. Holmes and Toshi Yoshihara, "When Comparing Navies, Measure Strength, Not Size," *Global Asia* 5, no. 4 (Winter 2010): 26–31.

79. Alfred Thayer Mahan, *Retrospect & Prospect: Studies in International Relations, Naval and Political* (Boston: Little, Brown, 1902), 164.

80. Alfred Thayer Mahan, "Retrospect upon the War between Japan and Russia," in *Naval Administration and Warfare* (Boston: Little, Brown, 1918), 133–73.

81. Wolfgang Wegener, *The Naval Strategy of the World War* (1929; repr., Annapolis, Md.: Naval Institute Press, 1989), 96–97.

82. Wegener, 103.

83. Wegener, 103.

84. Wegener, 104.

85. Friedrich Nietzsche, *The Will to Power*, trans. R. Kevin Hill and Michael A. Scarpitti (New York: Penguin, 2017).

86. Wegener, 97, 107.

87. James R. Holmes, "China Fashions a Maritime Identity," *Issues & Studies* 42, no. 3 (September 2006): 87–128.

Chapter 3. What Navies Do

1. Frans Osinga, *Science, Strategy and War: The Strategic Theory of John Boyd* (London: Routledge, 2007).

2. Instituting and managing change is a constant theme for Machiavelli, but he holds forth on change in republics and autocracies most pointedly in book 3, chapter 9 of his *Discourses* on Titus Livy's history of Rome. Niccolò Machiavelli, *Discourses on Livy*, trans. Harvey C. Mansfield and Nathan Tarcov (Chicago: University of Chicago Press, 1996), 239–41.

3. Eric Hoffer, *The Ordeal of Change* (1963; repr., Titus, N.J.: Hopewell, 2006). For a summary of Hoffer's views, see James R. Holmes, "A Longshoreman's Guide to Military Innovation," *National Interest*, March 22, 2016, https://nationalinterest.org/feature/longshoremans-guide-military-innovation-15562.

4. "War," writes Carl von Clausewitz, "is nothing but a duel on a larger scale. Countless duels go to make up war, but a picture of it as a whole can be formed by imagining a pair of wrestlers. Each tries through physical force to compel the other to do his will; his *immediate* aim is to *throw* his opponent in order to make him incapable of further resistance. *War is thus an act of force to compel our enemy to do our will*" (emphasis in original). The message from the Prussian master: respect the foe. Carl von Clausewitz, *On War*, trans. Michael Howard and Peter Paret (Princeton, N.J.: Princeton University Press, 1976), 75–77.

5. Henry A. Kissinger, *The Necessity for Choice* (New York: Harper, 1961), 12.

6. Ken Booth, *Navies and Foreign Policy* (London: Croom Helm, 1977), 15–17.

7. Clausewitz, *On War*, 94, 98, 216.

8. James R. Holmes, "'A Striking Thing': Leadership, Strategic Communications, and Roosevelt's Great White Fleet," *Naval War College Review* 61, no. 1 (Winter 2008): 51–67.

9. Sun Tzu, *The Illustrated Art of War*, trans. Samuel B. Griffith (1963; repr., Oxford: Oxford University Press, 2005), 115.

10. Clausewitz offers comfort even to weaker contestants: "Wars have in fact been fought between states of *very unequal strength, for actual war is often far removed from the pure concept postulated by theory*. Inability to carry on the struggle can, in practice, be replaced by two other grounds for making peace: the first is the improbability of victory; the second is its unacceptable cost" (my emphasis). Wise opponents can arrange matters to make victory seem improbable to their foes or its costs unacceptable. If successful, they prevail by default. Clausewitz, *On War*, 91.

11. Edward N. Luttwak, *The Political Uses of Sea Power* (Baltimore: Johns Hopkins University Press, 1974), 10–11.

12. Luttwak, 6.

13. Similarly, Clausewitz observes that commanders can hope to get their way through armed force in peacetime provided the *idea* of battle is present in all of the stakeholders' minds. If the idea of coercion is present, a contender may attain its goals without actually fighting for them. Combat, it seems, comes in many forms. This concept comes through most clearly in an older translation of *On War*. See Carl von Clausewitz, *On War*, trans. O. J. Matthijs Jolles (New York: Modern Library, 1943), 289–90. Luttwak, *Political Uses of Sea Power*, 11.

14. Luttwak, 11.

15. Luttwak, 11.

16. Luttwak, 6.

17. Luttwak, 14–15.

18. See James Cable, *Gunboat Diplomacy 1919–1991: Political Applications of Limited Naval Force*, rev. 3rd ed. (London: Palgrave Macmillan, 1994).

19. Richard McKenna, *The Sand Pebbles* (1962; repr., Annapolis, Md.: Naval Institute Press, 2001).

20. Kemp Tolley, *Yangtze Patrol: The U.S. Navy in China* (Annapolis, Md.: Naval Institute Press, 1971).

21. Luttwak, *Political Uses of Sea Power*, 28–34.

22. Luttwak, 41–43.

23. Luttwak, 43.

24. In the American context the police power derives from the Tenth Amendment to the U.S. Constitution.

25. Geoffrey Till, *Seapower: A Guide for the Twenty-First Century*, 3rd ed. (London: Routledge, 2013), 282–317.

26. U.S. Department of Defense, *Asia-Pacific Maritime Security Strategy*, 2015, Homeland Security Digital Library, accessed July 25, 2018, https://www.hsdl.org/?abstract&did=786636. The Trump administration has not yet issued such a directive but also has not disavowed the Obama strategy.

27. Robert W. Komer, *Bureaucracy Does Its Thing: Institutional Constraints on U.S.-GVN Performance in Vietnam* (Santa Monica: RAND Corporation, 1972).

28. Victor D. Cha, "Abandonment, Entrapment, and Neoclassical Realism in Asia: The United States, Japan, and Korea," *International Studies Quarterly* 44, no. 2 (June 2000): 261–91.

29. I review these dynamics in more depth in James R. Holmes, "Rough Waters for Coalition Building," in *Cooperation from Strength: The United States, China and the South China Sea*, ed. Patrick Cronin (Washington, D.C.: Center for a New American Security, 2012), 99–115.

30. Eyre Crowe, "Memorandum on the Present State of British Relations with France and Germany, January 1, 1907," in *British Documents on the*

Origins of the War 1898–1914, vol. 3: *The Testing of the Entente, 1904–6*, ed. G. P. Gooch and Harold Temperley (London: His Majesty's Stationery Office, 1927), 402–17.

31. Joseph S. Nye Jr., *Soft Power: The Means to Success in World Politics* (New York: Public Affairs, 2004).

32. David Galula, *Counterinsurgency Warfare: Theory and Practice* (New York: Praeger, 1964), 47–51.

33. Michele Flournoy and Shawn Brimley, "The Contested Commons," U.S. Naval Institute *Proceedings* 135, no. 7 (July 2009), https://www.usni.org/magazines/proceedings/2009-07/contested-commons. The coauthors pay tribute to Alfred Thayer Mahan for popularizing the concept of a marine common.

34. Hal Brands, "Paradoxes of the Gray Zone," FPRI E-Note, February 5, 2016, http://www.fpri.org/article/2016/02/paradoxes- gray-zone/.

35. Sam Bateman, "Solving the 'Wicked Problems' of Maritime Security: Are Regional Forums Up to the Task?" *Contemporary Southeast Asia* 33, no. 1 (2011): 1.

36. Bateman, 1.

37. "U.S. Concerned about Russia's Claim to Northern Sea Route—Pompeo," *Sputnik News*, May 6, 2019, https://sputniknews .com/europe/201905061074756096 -us-russia-claim-pompeo/; and "The Sea of Azov, a Ukraine-Russia Flashpoint," Agence France-Presse, November 26, 2018, https://news.yahoo .com/sea-azov-ukraine-russia-flashpoint-114438760.html.

38. Arsalan Shahla and Ladane Nasseri, "Iran Raises Stakes in U.S. Showdown with Threat to Close Hormuz," Bloomberg, April 22, 2019, https://www.bloomberg.com/news/articles/2019-04-22/iran-will-close-strait -of-hormuz-if-it-can-t-use-it-fars.

39. Clausewitz, *On War* (1976 ed.), 94, 98, 216.

40. Clausewitz, 605.

41. B. H. Liddell Hart, *Strategy*, 2nd rev. ed. (1954; repr., New York: Meridian, 1991), 338.

42. Liddell Hart, 332.

43. An excellent secondary account of U.S. grand strategy in the Asia-Pacific is Michael J. Green, *By More Than Providence: Grand Strategy and American Power in the Asia Pacific since 1783* (New York: Columbia University Press, 2017).

44. The term "recessional" comes from poet Rudyard Kipling, who wrote a poem by that name as an elegy for Britain's age of imperial mastery. Rudyard Kipling, "Recessional," July 17, 1897, Kipling Society Website, http://www .kiplingsociety.co.uk/poems_recess .htm. For more on the de facto handover of responsibility for the system, see Kori Schake, *Safe Passage: The Transition from British to American Hegemony* (Cambridge, Mass.: Harvard University Press, 2017); and Walter Russell Mead, *God and Gold: Britain, America, and the Making of the Modern World* (New York: Knopf, 2007).

45. Nicholas J. Spykman, *The Geography of the Peace*, ed. Helen R. Nicholl, intro. Frederick Sherwood Dunn (New York: Harcourt, Brace, 1943), 24–25.

46. J. C. Wylie, *Military Strategy: A General Theory of Power Control* (1967; repr., Annapolis, Md.: Naval Institute Press, 1989), 34.

47. Harold Sprout and Margaret Sprout, *The Rise of American Naval Power* (Princeton, N.J.: Princeton University Press, 1944), 202–22. See also Margaret Sprout's wonderful essay on Mahan: Margaret Sprout, "Mahan: Evangelist of Sea Power," in *Makers of Modern Strategy*, ed. Edward Meade Earle (Princeton, N.J.: Princeton University Press, 1943), 415–45.

48. Alfred Thayer Mahan, *Influence of Sea Power upon History, 1660–1783* (1890; repr., New York: Dover, 1987), 79.

49. Julian S. Corbett, *Some Principles of Maritime Strategy*, intro. Eric J. Grove (1911; repr., Annapolis, Md.: Naval Institute Press, 1988), 16.

50. The U.S. Department of Defense defines "joint" as connoting "activities, operations, organizations, etc., in which elements of two or more Military Departments participate." U.S. Department of Defense, *DOD Dictionary of Military and Associated Terms*, June 2018, 123, http://www.jcs.mil/Portals/36/Documents/Doctrine/pubs/dictionary.pdf.

51. Corbett, *Some Principles of Maritime Strategy*, 16. How Corbett phrases this passage has always puzzled me. Why designate "the fear of" what the fleet makes it possible for the army to do as the determining factor rather than what the fleet actually helps the army do in action? This peculiar wording offers a reminder not to treat even classic works as sacred writ. Even the greats make the occasional misstep.

52. Mahan, *Influence of Sea Power upon History*, 365–74.

53. Mahan, 365–74.

54. Alfred Thayer Mahan, *The Influence of Sea Power upon the French Revolution and Empire, 1793–1812*, 2 vols. (Boston: Little, Brown, 1892).

55. Alfred Thayer Mahan, *Sea Power in Its Relations to the War of 1812*, 2 vols. (Boston: Little, Brown, 1905); and Mahan, *Influence of Sea Power upon the French Revolution and Empire*.

56. Quoted in Eric J. Grove, Introduction to *Some Principles of Maritime Strategy*, by Julian S. Corbett (1911; repr., Annapolis, Md.: Naval Institute Press, 1988), xxix.

57. Frank McLynn, *1759: The Year Britain Became Master of the World* (New York: Grove Atlantic, 2005).

58. Russell F. Weigley, *The American Way of War: A History of United States Military Strategy and Policy* (Bloomington: Indiana University Press, 1973), 21.

59. Corbett, *Some Principles of Maritime Strategy*, 323–24.

60. Corbett, 91.

61. Corbett, 94.

62. Corbett, 115.

63. Corbett, 115.

64. Corbett, 104.

65. Corbett, 102–3.

66. Samuel Eliot Morison, *The Two-Ocean War: A Short History of the United States Navy in the Second World War* (New York: Galahad, 1963), 183.

67. Corbett, *Some Principles of Maritime Strategy*, 234.

68. Corbett, 161–63.

69. Corbett, 158.

70. It is worth pointing out that Chinese Communist Party chairman Mao Zedong fashioned a virtually identical concept of active defense around the same time— and even called it the same thing. Active defense remains the lodestone of Chinese military and maritime strategy to this day. See M. Taylor Fravel, *Active Defense: China's Military Strategy since 1949* (Princeton, N.J.: Princeton University Press, 2019).

71. Corbett, *Some Principles of Maritime Strategy,* 210, 310–11.

72. Corbett, 310–11.

73. Corbett, 310–11.

74. Corbett, 212–19.

75. Corbett, 215.

76. Corbett, 212–19.

77. As indeed they might. Chinese strategists are avid readers of Mahan's works, but they also consult Corbett. James R. Holmes and Toshi Yoshihara, "China's Navy: A Turn to Corbett?" U.S. Naval Institute *Proceedings* 136, no. 12 (December 2010), https://www.usni.org/magazines/proceedings/2010-12/chinas -navy-turn-corbett.

78. Toshi Yoshihara, Testimony before the U.S.-China Economic and Security Review Commission Hearing on "China's Offensive Missile Forces," April 1, 2015, U.S.-China Commission Web site, https://www.uscc.gov/sites/default/ files/Yoshihara%20USCC%20Testimony%201%20April%202015.pdf.

79. Craig Symonds, *World War II at Sea* (Oxford: Oxford University Press, 2018), 85–88.

80. Corbett, *Some Principles of Maritime Strategy*, 132.

81. Larrie D. Ferreiro, "Mahan and the 'English Club' of Lima, Peru: The Genesis of *The Influence of Sea Power upon History*," *Journal of Military History* 72, no. 3 (July 2008): 901–6.

82. Corbett, *Some Principles of Maritime Strategy*, 15–16.

83. Wylie, *Military Strategy*, 22–23.

84. Wylie, 23.

85. Wylie, 25.

86. Wylie, 25.

87. Corbett, *Some Principles of Maritime Strategy*, 60–67.

88. David Gates, *The Spanish Ulcer: A History of the Peninsular War* (Boston: Da Capo, 2001).

89. See, for instance, Headquarters, Department of the Army, Field Manual 3-24.2, *Tactics in Counterinsurgency*, April 2009, https://fas.org/irp/doddir /army/fm3-24-2.pdf; Fred Kaplan, *The Insurgents: David Petraeus and the Plot to Change the American Way of War* (New York: Simon & Schuster, 2013); U.S.

Marine Corps, *Small Wars Manual 1940* (Washington, D.C.: Government Printing Office, 1940); and David Galula, *Counterinsurgency Warfare: Theory and Practice* (1964; repr., Westport, Conn.: Praeger, 2006).

90. David C. Evans and Mark R. Peattie, *Kaigun: Strategy, Tactics, and Technology in the Imperial Japanese Navy, 1887–1941* (Annapolis, Md.: Naval Institute Press, 1997), 150–51.

91. Adm. John Richardson, the chief of naval operations from 2015–2019, forbade naval officialdom to use the acronym "A2/AD" to describe China's maritime military strategy. CNO Richardson believes the acronym oversimplifies, connoting a strategy that blocks U.S. forces out of contested zones altogether. There are no absolute no-go zones. For instance, maps of Asia displaying aircraft and missile ranges from Chinese coastlines convey the impression that nothing survives that comes within weapons range. This exaggerates the capabilities of any local defender. Christopher P. Cavas, "CNO Bans 'A2AD' as Jargon," *Defense News*, October 3, 2016, https://www.defensenews.com/naval/2016/10/04/cno-bans-a2ad-as-jargon/.

92. Arthur Waldron, *The Great Wall of China: From History to Myth* (1990; repr., Cambridge: Cambridge University Press, 2002).

93. I have likened access denial to the "crumple zone" in automobiles, a sacrificial component designed to collapse in a controlled way upon impact—thus shielding the passengers, whose safety is the main concern, from external harm. James R. Holmes, "Visualize Chinese Sea Power," U.S. Naval Institute *Proceedings* 144, no. 6 (June 2018): 26–31.

94. The concept dates to antiquity. For instance, Mahan commented on Syracusan alternatives for inhibiting Athenian maritime access to Sicily in the fifth century BC. Alfred Thayer Mahan, *Naval Strategy Compared and Contrasted with the Principles and Practice of Military Operations on Land* (Boston: Little, Brown, 1911), 223–31. See also Sam J. Tangredi, *Anti-Access Warfare: Countering A2/AD Strategies* (Annapolis, Md.: Naval Institute Press, 2013).

95. I review Mahan's commentary on the fortress fleet and contend that China's military has refreshed the idea and put it into practice. See James R. Holmes, "When China Rules the Sea," *Foreign Policy*, September 23, 2015, https://foreignpolicy.com/2015/09/23/when-china-rules-the-sea-navy-xi-jinping-visit/; and "A Fortress Fleet for China," *Whitehead Journal of Diplomacy* 11, no. 2 (Summer/Fall 2010): 19–32.

96. Theodore Ropp, "Continental Doctrines of Sea Power," in *Makers of Modern Strategy: Military Thought from Machiavelli to Hitler*, ed. Edward Meade Earle (Princeton, N.J.: Princeton University Press, 1943), 446–56.

97. For more, see James R. Holmes, "Great Red Fleet: How China Was Inspired by Teddy Roosevelt," *National Interest*, October 30, 2017, https://nationalinterest.org/feature/great-red-fleet-how-china-was-inspired-by-teddy-roosevelt-22968.

98. On one vision of joint sea power, see Toshi Yoshihara and James R. Holmes, "Asymmetric Warfare, American Style," U.S. Naval Institute *Proceedings* 138, no. 4 (April 2012), https://www.usni.org/magazines/proceedings/2012-04/asymmetric-warfare-american-style; James R. Holmes, "Defend the First Island Chain," U.S. Naval Institute *Proceedings* 140, no. 4 (April 2014), https://www.usni.org/magazines/proceedings/2014-04/defend-first-island-chain; and Andrew Krepinevich, "How to Deter China," *Foreign Affairs*, March/April 2015, https://www.foreignaffairs.com/articles/china/2015-02-16/how-deter-china.

99. Max Weber, *Economy and Society: An Outline of Interpretive Sociology*, ed. Guenther Roth and Claus Wittich, trans. Ephraim Fischoff et al., 3 vols. (New York: Bedminster Press, 1968), 223, 973–93.

100. Komer, *Bureaucracy Does Its Thing*.

101. Andrew F. Krepinevich Jr., *The Army and Vietnam* (Baltimore: Johns Hopkins University Press, 1988).

102. Irving L. Janis, *Groupthink: Psychological Studies of Policy Decisions and Fiascoes* (Boston: Cengage, 1982).

103. Corbett, *Some Principles of Maritime Strategy*, 164, 167.

104. Bernard Brodie, *Strategy in the Missile Age* (Princeton, N.J.: Princeton University Press, 1959), 26–27.

105. Edmund Burke, *Reflections on the French Revolution*, vol. 24, part 3, Harvard Classics (New York: P. F. Collier & Son, 1909–14) accessed at Bartleby.com, https://www.bartleby.com/24/3/12 .html.

106. Andrew Gordon, *The Rules of the Game: Jutland and British Naval Command* (1997; repr., Annapolis, Md.: Naval Institute Press, 2000).

107. Gordon, 155–92.

108. Samuel P. Huntington, "National Policy and the Transoceanic Navy," U.S. Naval Institute *Proceedings* 80, no. 5 (May 1954), https://www.usni.org/magazines/proceedings/1954-05/national-policy-and-transoceanic-navy.

109. " . . . From the Sea" appeared the same year that political scientist Francis Fukuyama declared an end to political history, contending that all forms of government had been tried out and liberal democracy was best. It is hard not to suspect sea-service leaders were swept up in the triumphalism accompanying the end of the Cold War, just as Fukuyama and many others were. The nature of the Cold War's denouement—complete victory in a global superpower struggle without fighting—may well have exacerbated the problem. Francis Fukuyama, *The End of History and the Last Man* (1992; repr. New York: Free Press, 2006).

110. U.S. Navy and Marine Corps, " . . . From the Sea: Preparing the Naval Service for the 21st Century," September 1992, U.S. Navy Web site, http://www.navy.mil/navydata/policy/from sea/fromsea.txt.

111. No education in military or political affairs is complete without the ancients. For starters, see Herodotus, *The Histories*, trans. Tom Holland, intro. Paul

Cartledge (London: Penguin Classics, 2013); and Thucydides, *The War of the Peloponnesians and the Athenians*, ed. Jeremy Mynott (Cambridge: Cambridge University Press, 2013).

112. U.S. Naval War College Public Affairs, "Nimitz Diary Unveils Naval War College Legacy of Learning," February 26, 2014, U.S. Navy Web site, http://www.navy.mil/submit/display.asp?story_id=79354.

113. Ernest Hemingway, *Men at War* (1942; repr., New York: Random House, 1982), 8–15.

Index

abandonment, police functions of navies and, 106–7

access denial: as active defense, 139–42; as crumple zone in automobiles, 166n93; debate over, 138; history of, 166n94; Richardson on China's, 166n91; shore batteries and, 85; T. Roosevelt on, 143–44;

active defense: access denial as form of, 139–40; balking a stronger enemy's strategy with, 131–32; Corbett on, 130–31; *jeune école* and fortress fleet and, 142–43; Mao's concept of, 165n70

air theories of war, 21, 22

aircraft carriers: as capital ships, 80; fleet size and power statistics and, 86–87; infrastructure of U.S. naval power and, 133; naval aviation in World War II and, 79–80; nuclear-powered, refueling by, 55; Panama Canal practice raids by, 154–55n62; submarines compared with, 81; U-boats in the Atlantic and, 77; U.S., after Pearl Harbor, 37

airplanes: sea as three-dimensional domain for, 18–21. *See also* aviators

Alexander the Great, 14

ancients, Greek and Roman: education in military or political fairs and, 167–68n111; on rejecting hubris, 149–50. *See also* Athens; Sparta; *specific writers*

antiship ballistic and cruise missiles, 80, 133

Archidamus, 3

Arctic Ocean, 21, 27

area denial: debate over, 138; shore batteries and, 85. *See also* access denial

Army, U.S., conventional warfare and, 145

Asia and Asia Pacific region: Mercator projections of Americas and, 59–60; problems in, 113–14. *See also* China; India; Indo-Pacific; Japan; South China Sea; Taiwan

Asia-Pacific Maritime Security Strategy (Obama administration, 2015), 105

Athens: access denial to Sicily for, 166n94; economics and finance in war against Sparta by, 3. *See also* ancients, Greek and Roman

Atlantic, Battles of, 77

Atlantic Conveyor, 76

Aube, Théophile, 142

automobiles, crumple zone in, access denial as, 166n93

aviators: naval, eclipsing surface combatants, 79; sea as environment molding, 21–22; three-dimensional view of earth's surface by, 58. *See also* air theories of war; airplanes

About the Author

James R. Holmes is J. C. Wylie Chair of Maritime Strategy at the Naval War College and a former U.S. Navy engineering and gunnery officer. He formerly served on the faculty of the University of Georgia School of Public and International Affairs.